POLICE SHOTGUN MANUAL

POLICE SHOTGUN MANUAL

How to Survive
Against All Odds

Bill Clede

Photos by author unless otherwise credited.
Photos in gun and accessory sections were
supplied by manufacturers.

Stackpole Books

Copyright © 1986 by Bill Clede

Published by
STACKPOLE BOOKS
Cameron and Kelker Streets
P.O. Box 1831
Harrisburg, PA 17105

Printed in the U.S.A.

Library of Congress Cataloging-in-Publication Data

Clede, Bill.
    Police shotgun manual.

    Bibliography: p.
    1. Police—Equipment and supplies. 2. Shotguns. 3. Shooting
I. Title.
HV7936.E7C54   1986   363.2′32′028   86-948
ISBN 0-8117-1350-4

Contents

Acknowledgments

Many people helped make this book timely and thorough. Most are quoted in appropriate places, but some deserve special recognition.

Bob Hunt, Jerry Lane, and Bill Burroughs of the Smith & Wesson Academy ran me through two weeks of training, then patiently posed for pictures. Jerry Lane has since gone with Heckler & Koch to establish a training academy in Virginia. Massad Ayoob, Lethal Force Institute, gave me the benefit of his extensive research and ideas. John Farnum, Defense Training, added more for me to think about. Bob Lindsey, now training director for Wells Fargo Guard Services, developed the techniques for retaining the shoulder weapon and he directed the photography; so we know it's right. Gun writer Brook Elliott tested the BRI slugs and it's because of him they are included. Norm Wilson of Remington conducted a clinic to show the value of skeet to police shotgun training. I could list several hundred members of the International Association of Law Enforcement Firearms Instructors who, at the National Training Conferences and in correspondence, offered ideas, tips, and encouragement.

Most of the manufacturers were helpful, but you can be sure some of the comments concerning them and their products will be outdated by the time this book is published. Changes often occur quickly in the firearms industry, and it is sometimes difficult to keep up with them — in print.

You Can Do It

As the challenges facing law enforcement officers change, the equipment needed to do the job also changes. With the increasing incidence of worldwide terrorism, the policeman today may face an armed and well-trained raiding party of radicals rather than a lone criminal. England, which armed its Bobbies only with truncheons, is discreetly arming certain officers. In the United States, where officers were once issued only a sidearm, shotguns are playing a more prominent role. Rather than being "special weapons" reserved for tactical units, the shotgun is now part of the basic patrol equipment.

It is no longer unusual to see officers responding to an "armed" situation call, shotgun in hand.

Because of this, firearms training programs are changing. Not only are new shooting techniques being developed to make the officer more effective with his handgun, but new shotgun techniques are also being developed and are being given greater prominence in the training schedule.

The shotgun's application in tactical situations is having its greatest renaissance since World War I.

It is not difficult to become proficient with the shotgun.

The last of the gun industry's great exhibition shooters was the late Herb Parsons. He replaced the aging Ad Topperwein on the shooting circuit for Winchester-Western in the 1930s, and traveled the country giving an average of three shooting exhibitions a week, fifty weeks a year. In the 1940s he gave 238 exhibitions for soldiers at military installations, and he served as a gunnery instructor during the war.

Just to give you an idea of what he could do with a shotgun:

Parsons would bend over like a football center and toss a handful of eggs between his legs; then he'd turn with his shotgun and scramble them one at a time. He'd take seven clay targets and toss them high into the air; then break them one at a time with a 12-gauge Winchester Model 12 before they hit the ground. An idiosyncrasy of that gun was that you could hold the trigger back and pump the action for rapid fire.

He would joke with his audiences, "They're not hard to hit, folks, just awfully easy to miss."

Born in Somerville, Tennessee, Parsons was the only man I knew who could crack such an old gag as, "Save your Confederate money, folks. The South will rise again," and make his audience laugh at it.

For many years, he was a perennial member of the Sports Afield Trap and Skeet All-American teams. But he was the first to say that his unique talent was nothing that any normally healthy man couldn't duplicate — if he shot as much as Herb Parsons did. In the late 1950s, I was the guy in the Shooting Promotion Department who scheduled Parsons' shows, so we had a number of occasions to talk.

Most of you are not out to become exhibition shooters, but Herb Parsons proves the point that practice — getting to know your gun — is what it takes to become a good shot.

Your biggest problem is getting experience with that shotgun stashed in the gunlock of your police cruiser.

The best suggestion I can offer is to hunt with it — provided department regulations will allow you to do so. For upland gamebirds with birdshot, or deer with rifled slugs (where it is permitted), the short barrel shotgun is a convenient sporting gun. Try that riot gun on the skeet field at your local gun club, with appropriate loads. You'd be surprised how well you can do with it.

In the bargain, you will get to know your duty gun — which is extremely important.

Obviously, you cannot learn to shoot by reading a book. But it can give you an understanding of the techniques your instructor teaches on the range. The importance of this book lies in its exposure to new ideas in shotgun shooting techniques. If it makes you think — and practice — you will become a better shooter. Try the various techniques. See what works best for you.

Good luck!

Bill Clede

1

Deadliest Gun in the West

The stories on television and in the movies always show the policeman with his sidearm and the SWAT officer with his M-16. Western movies depict the frontier lawman with his Colt Peacemaker and Winchester 73. But there is another gun whose very presence struck fear into the heart of the bravest lawbreaker.

The well-armed lawman of the 1880s was described by Wyatt Earp himself.

"Good or bad," he said, "the gunslinger belted two Colt 45's on his hips, strapped his Winchester lever-action rifle in a scabbard on the right side of his saddle and, with a leather thong, hung a sawed-off shotgun from the saddle horn."

Today, the well-armed lawman has one four-inch .357 Magnum revolver (or a 14-shot 9mm pistol), speedloaders (or clips) on his belt, and a shotgun in a gunlock within easy reach. The handgun is handy. But when the chips are down you reach for the shotgun.

Doc Holliday is remembered for his favorite weapon, and with good reason. When he joined Morgan, Virgil, and Wyatt Earp on their way to the OK Corral in October 1881, Doc Holliday carried the most formidable weapon he could find for the purpose. Each barrel of his sawed-off, 10-gauge Greener double barrel shotgun held eighteen big pellets of buckshot — each bigger than a .32 caliber bullet.

Of the six gunmen killed in that showdown gunfight, Tom Lowery, who took both barrels of Holliday's double gun, was the only one who did not fight back after he was hit.

Sheriff Pat Garrett set the pattern for modern law enforcement officers. He carried a short shotgun in his buggy in much the same manner as you pack your riot gun — standing vertically in a special bracket with the butt down, just to the right of the driver.

There were three reasons for the popularity of the shotgun in the Old West: its power at short range, its versatility, and its ease of pointing. A man didn't have to practice for hours to hit a bandit at 30 paces. One man, armed with a shotgun, could sweep an alleyway clean — even in the dark.

The homesteader used his shotgun for many purposes. Loaded with bird-shot, it put prairie chicken or quail in the oven. Loaded with a "pumpkin ball," he could bag a deer at 75 yards. Loaded with buckshot, it turned his cabin into a well-armed fortress. The first two purposes are just as valid today, according to many sportsmen. The third purpose is mighty important to you, as a law enforcement officer.

The power of the shotgun at short range is awesome. A single pellet hits with a force dependent on its velocity and mass. Add another and the two hit twice as hard? No, *more*. As the number of hits doubles, some experts argue that the force of the total impact is *quadrupled*.

A hunter friend, Roy Sanden, told me of his experience of being hit by a charge of birdshot — several hundred tiny pellets — that failed to penetrate his heavy clothing. "But I was slammed to the ground thirty feet away as though I'd been hit by a car," he told me.

The popularity of the unglorified shotgun is evident when you consider its persistence in modern-day language. The youngster riding beside the driver in a hot rod is "riding shotgun" like the guard on a Wells Fargo stagecoach. When the oilmen of Texas and Oklahoma needed protection they hired a "shotgun man." The miners of Gold Rush days hired "shotgun guards" to protect their claims. Honest miners in Alaska complained of "shotgun ruffians." And who hasn't heard of a "shotgun wedding"?

The desperado who would think nothing of facing up to a sixgun, would think twice when he heard the ominous "clack-clack" of those big hammers being cocked on a double gun. Nowadays, the sound is a "rack-rack" of the pump gun action loading the chamber. And the big black hole of a 12-gauge muzzle looks like the entrance to hell itself, when you're on the wrong end of it.

Writing about Bat Masterson, Richard O'Connor said, "The shotgun played a larger role in taming frontier towns than may be imagined. It was one weapon that gave pause to the most confident of gunmen. The mental picture of his guts being strewn on the ground at a never-miss range was enough to cool off almost any hothead. Many a peace officer . . . relied more on the shotgun as a pacifier than the more publicized six-shooter."

The times and the laws may be different now, but the principles are just as true today as they ever were. When you know you're going into a potentially hot situation, the gun in your hands should be the shotgun. Your handgun is a "defensive" weapon. The shotgun is undoubtedly an "offensive" weapon, far more effective within pistol-shot range than any handgun ever thought of being.

With one 12-gauge shotgun, you've got buckshot that does the same thing as your pistol—times nine—each time you pull the trigger. You can use a rifled slug load to punch through a barricade to reach the felon shooting at you from behind "cover." Or you can lob a tear gas grenade to disperse a mob; or shoot a little finned projectile through the window glass to put tear gas into a hideout room or automobile.

The shotgun is versatile, effective, and a bit more tolerant of your marksmanship. But you've got to be familiar with your shotgun if you want it to serve *your* purpose properly.

2

Police Aren't Just Pistols

The policeman is always pictured with his pistol, but there's an arsenal of *alternate* weapons that he uses as tools of his trade.

Our local television news station recently showed teams of policemen scouring the neighborhood for a guy who blew away his ex-girlfriend after an argument and then escaped on foot. Most of the cops were carrying shotguns. And from what I could tell on the tube, the guns were loaded, actions closed, and I hope the safeties were "on."

The situation ended without incident, probably because it happened shortly after an earlier situation that had dire consequences for that city.

2.1 A Preventable Error

The radio call put cars on the lookout for a vehicle used in an armed robbery. State Police chased a car matching the make and model, even to the number and description of occupants. City police stopped it, surrounded the vehicle. One city officer was holding his shotgun while another checked out the occupants. The shotgun discharged, accidentally, as a Firearms Review Board later determined. The city is presently supporting the now-paraplegic victim for the rest of his life. He and his companions were not the ones involved in the crime.

Lt. Steve Knibloe of the East Windsor (Conn.) Police Department simulates searching for an armed adversary. His shotgun has a pistol grip but it's at the ready, should he need it in a hurry. If it discharged accidentally, the shot would go in the air.

The furor that followed asked such questions as, "How familiar was the officer with the shotgun?" and "How well trained was he in handling the shotgun he was issued?"

The answers were embarrassing. Part of the court settlement was that city officers now have to qualify four times a year.

The shotgun is a patrol weapon, one used by the patrol officer rather than one relegated to specially trained tactical units. There are new shooting techniques that enable you to employ the shotgun effectively, efficiently and safely. Yet, it seems we expect everyone to be born with the skill of shooting a shotgun.

2.2 Inadequate Training — Potential Liability

"The instructor used dummy rounds to show us how to load and unload the shotgun. Then he said a few words about pointing it. On the range we fired five 00 Buck and five slugs at silhouettes. It wasn't until a later 'qualifying' session that we fired birdshot at flying clay targets."

This example isn't hypothetical. Was that the extent of your first shotgun training? It was mine, but not at my present department. Too many officers have described this case to me as their introduction to the shotgun. Because of inadequate shotgun training, municipalities have paid a dear price for not keeping up with the times.

In the unintentional shooting example above, the officer was obviously doing all the wrong things: holding the gun dead on the suspect, his finger on the trigger, the safety off. Had he been taught the gun handling and shooting techniques I learned in the Shotgun Instructor course at the Smith & Wesson Academy, the gun would not have fired. Even if it had, the shot would have gone over the guy's head.

The officer would have been saved the trauma and anguish of having crippled an innocent man. His city would have been saved more money than a good training program would cost over the next twenty years — or however long that victim lives.

A survey among state's attorneys raised the question of the possible liability of a "second" handgun. This consensus is just as pertinent to the shotgun. None saw any greater liability potential than with the primary duty handgun, *provided the officer is trained in its use.* They all agreed that lack of training incurs liability. Too, inadequate training could incur liability, as it did in the case cited. All training procedures must be relevant to the situations the individual officers face.

2.3 Why Not a Submachine Gun?

That's a good question. I'm sure my aversion to submachine guns stems from my not being able to shoot well with them. But there is a better answer.

The submachine gun has its place. If you're 50–100 yards away trying to cover the advance of your partner, the submachine gun can't be beat. You can drop more bullets, more quickly, and more accurately "way out there" than you can with any other gun.

But just how often do you expect to lay a cover-fire barrage in your neighborhood?

If you're within 25 yards, the advantage goes to the shotgun. You've got, say, seven 00 Buck loads in your gun. You can pump out seven shots in just a few seconds. But remember, each shot propels nine .33 caliber pellets toward the target. You're actually shooting sixty-three bullets.

How long would it take you to blurt out sixty-three rounds from a submachine gun and put them where they're supposed to go? You'd have to change magazines at least once.

The firepower potential of the shotgun is awesome, within its designed range.

We found a piece of half-inch plywood at the range. It had a few .22 caliber holes in it, but we ignored them. We propped the panel up with a stake and fired a skeet load into it from about fifteen feet away just to see what it

At 10 feet, the main force of the birdshot pattern in the center blew a big hole clean through the half-inch plywood. The pellets on the fringe of the tight pattern entered the wood.

would do. There was about a two-inch hole right through it and a six-inch area of freckles where pellets went into the plywood so deep you couldn't see them.

If birdshot does that much damage, what would 00 Buck do? Nine .33 caliber balls penetrated the plywood. Even the plastic wad was protruding out the back side of the wood.

If the perpetrator is hiding behind a car door, your .357 or 9mm *may* get through to him, but it is not likely. You can be sure that a 12-gauge rifled slug will penetrate one door, go through him and probably the door on the other side, too.

In any normal police operation I'd ever expect to be involved in — patrol, surveillance, raid, or riot — the shotgun has it all over any other kind of gun. Leave the submachine guns to the military.

2.4 Purpose of Training

The purpose of training is to instill in you the habits you need to stay alive and out of trouble on the street. If you get five shells to shoot at a silhouette and aren't shown *how,* is that training? We might test your ability to put five shots onto a target as part of qualification but that's not training.

Training takes time. It takes drilling you in an action so much that you start doing it without thinking about it. Training must be designed so that the

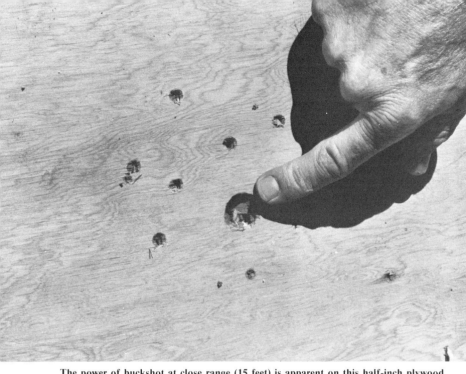

The power of buckshot at close range (15 feet) is apparent on this half-inch plywood panel. Each of the nine pellets penetrated. Even the plastic wad entered the panel, and protruded out the other side.

habits you develop are good habits, not necessarily convenient ones. The infamous Newhall incident in California taught us that you will react on the street exactly the way you were trained on the range.

If your instructor can't take the time he wants with you on the range, who stands to gain if you get some extra training and supervised practice on your own? You know who!

It's vital that you understand how important it is for you to know your shotgun, understand its function, and feel comfortable handling it safely — and effectively.

3

Attitudes: His and Yours

When you pick up a shotgun, you know you've got an "offensive" weapon. It takes forethought to arm yourself with a shotgun. Your handgun is by your side all the time. It is your weapon of ultimate *defense*. You don't have to plan for it. You don't even have to think about it, if you've practiced enough to make your reactions instinctive.

But the shotgun's a different story.

You have the shotgun in hand only when it's called for in a situation of potential deadly threat — an armed felon runs into the woods, is holed up in a hideaway, or an angry mob moves against you. You push the button to release the gunlock and you grab the weapon that gives you far greater firepower than the handgun.

You've made a decision. But are you ready to implement it?

3.1 The Criminal's Attitude

If you've spent time on the street, I don't have to tell you that the criminal isn't like your average citizen. He doesn't think the same way we do. He doesn't have the same attitudes. If you're new to this business, it helps to better understand what it is you're up against.

It really doesn't matter what the sociologists and psychiatrists say. Both have studied the criminal mind and environment to determine "causes" and develop "treatments," and each seems to have his own pet theories. But I don't care *why* some guy is trying to blow me away. It matters only that he *is*.

You'd better believe that his intentions aren't benevolent. He isn't going to change his mind out of pity for your wife and family. He will change his mind *only* if it means his own survival.

The criminal attitude develops early in life, probably in all of us. The most embarrassing moment in my life was when my mother made me pay the grocer for the five cookies I'd snitched from the cookie jar. But such lessons are learned by most of us early in life. For a few, they have an opposite effect. I know twin brothers who grew up in the ghetto of a large city. One is a sergeant on the police department and well respected by his fellows. The other is the antithesis of all that is good, and is not above dealing in drugs.

The other day I assisted in the arrest of a group of six kids who entered our town on four bicycles, obviously looking for two more bicycles. A citizen saw one of them take a bicycle from in front of a grocery store and called the police. The boys were stopped about a mile away by police officers in three cruisers. The one on the stolen bike gave us his name. But it wasn't the name on his birth certificate. He figured he could use a choice of names because his mother had been married several times.

"They (criminals) regard human beings who conform to society as a resource, to be harvested like corn or complacent livestock," says Massad Ayoob, a prolific writer on police subjects. He tells the story of Ronnie, a 29-year-old professional burglar and car thief.

Ronnie has stolen some 1,400 cars and burgled more than 300 carefully selected homes. He's a model prisoner on the inside but, outside the walls, he's a different breed.

"I never did a job without a gun in my belt," Ronnie says, "and if anyone had ever tried to stop me, I would have killed him."

The only things that scare Ronnie are a house with *two* Dobermans and a homeowner who looks like he knows how to use the gun he's holding, according to Ayoob.

"I don't even think of criminals as predatory animals," Ayoob explains. "Spend time with animals and you can relate with them. From the public's point of view, the best analogy is with werewolves. Until you meet one, they simply don't exist.

"Psychiatrists call them sociopaths. They don't really care about other people one way or the other. They steal your belongings the way you devour an ear of corn, feeling good afterward for having sated their appetite, and with absolutely no regard for the feelings of the cornstalk.

"The sociopath feels the same justifications as a soldier during wartime," Ayoob continues. "He serves the greater good of *himself.* The suffering of his victims is simply *their* problem."

3.2 The Cop's Attitude

When you fire a gun, your *only* purpose is to stop the aggressor before he kills or maims you or another person. Think about it. The need to shoot is really determined by the actions of the criminal. Your shooting "decision" is really a split-second *recognition* of the circumstances presented to you. Capability, opportunity, and jeopardy are the elements of a shooting decision. When all three are present, you have no decision.

Obviously, threat–response isn't that cut and dried. It's a scale of force exerted according to the force exerted against you.

There are alternatives to deadly force. If you are well trained in Defensive Tactics, you have more alternatives than if you aren't. But when you face the ultimate threat, your response is obviously ultimate.

The problem is that "routine" patrol dulls your senses, makes you complacent. And carelessness has gotten guys killed.

I'll bet you know people who think that "poor victim of society" really doesn't mean to harm anybody with the gun he's holding. (Maybe the gun is tucked into waistband behind his back where you can't see it.) Why he's just a burglar, not a killer. Tell that to Ronnie, the burglar Massad Ayoob interviewed.

Besides, burglary is just a property crime, isn't it?

"Three-fifths of all rapes, three-fifths of all robberies, and about one-third of all aggravated and simple assaults are committed by burglars," according to a 1985 Bureau of Justice Statistics study. In 30 percent of the incidents where a burglar was confronted by a household member, a violent crime was committed.

Bureau Director Steven R. Schlessinger said that household burglary "ranks among the more serious felony crimes, not only because it involves the illegal entry of one's home, but also because a substantial proportion of the violent crimes that occur in the home take place during a burglary.

"Thus, burglary is potentially a far more serious crime than its classification as a property offense indicates," he explained. "For many victims, including those who avoid the trauma of personal confrontation, the invasion of one's home produces permanent emotional scars."

Think about that the next time you answer a "burglary-in-progress" call.

Too many of us grew up in policing with the attitude that "It won't happen to me." Firearms training is "target practice." The gun is a symbol, like the badge. Such an attitude leads to suffering aggravated consequences of Post-Shooting Trauma.

It's not a question of "if" you ever have to use a gun. It's more a matter of "when." You'll suffer the shock and sadness afterwards. But if you are mentally prepared for the time when you have to shoot, you can more easily cope with the trauma. The gun cannot be ignored. It's a fact of life. Even though you'd never want to harm a soul, your gun waits on call and your skill with it could save someone's life, *perhaps your own.*

3.3 Use Discretion

There are times when discretion is the better part of valor. It is trite but true that "Fools rush in where Angels fear to tread."

In an officer survival course I attended, the "final exam" was a one-on-one scenario. "It's a 'man with gun' call and there's no backup available. You have to go into the building by yourself." That sets up why you violate the first rule of survival.

Through the door, you're in a long hallway. Boxes and junk are strewn all along it. There's a bare bulb hanging down behind you. No, I didn't think to unscrew it. One demerit. But I remembered to use cover, as I slowly made my way from one hiding place to another. I rushed past one big carton without checking to see what was behind it. Two demerits.

I finally reached the end of the hallway. Stairs went up to a landing, turned and continued up to the second floor. The stairs were dark. But it was some 30 feet, bathed in light, from the last good cover behind a motor generator to the foot of the dark stairs.

Turning to the instructor behind me, I said, "There's no way I can go beyond this point and survive."

"What's your decision?" he asked.

"I stop right here and wait him out."

At the critique, the instructor explained they had purposely set up a "no-win" situation. It goes against the grain of a macho cop to "back off." That's not the same as "backing down." It turned out that I was the only one in class who survived the test.

3.4 But Never Give Up

Did you play tag as a kid? When you're tagged, you're done. Police training scenarios follow similar rules. The hostile target pops out and you don't kill it. You're dead.

Even stronger than the sex drive, the survival instinct can fight incredible adversity. We've all heard war stories of hyped-up commandos running through a hail of bullets to kill an adversary. One sergeant took 13 hits from a machine gun, killed the gunner, and survived. A soldier took one hit in a very private part of his body. Hardly a fatal wound. But he died. He lost his will to survive.

Remember, four out of five shootings do not disable the one who's shot.

When you are shot, it's no game of tag. It doesn't necessarily put you out of action. It should make you angry. So *take the offensive.* Why let some scumbag spoil your day? When someone of his ilk inflicts a nondisabling injury on you, you should feel totally justified in using the shotgun to stop his felonious assault.

4

History of the Shotgun

If you were interested in the development of firearms, you'd be a gun collector and know more about it than I do. Besides, there are books galore on gun history, historic guns, and people who used guns in founding our great nation. We needn't duplicate those treatises here. But there's always a chance you'll be put in position of having to render a strange gun harmless. For example, a senile subject may think the Indians are attacking his cabin and he grabs granddad's old heirloom out of the attic to fend off all comers.

Once such a situation is cooled, someone has to make sure the old fowling piece isn't going to hurt anyone. (All policemen are gun experts, you know.)

These old guns can hurt — and sometimes do. I read of an accident some years ago when two kids were playing in the attic with an old percussion lock muzzleloader they had found there. They decided it would be fun to play Dan'l Boone. The kid with the gun managed to get it cocked. He aimed it at his playmate and pulled the trigger.

Now, that gun had lain in repose for at least 100 years. It had probably hung over a mantle for many years before it was put out of sight and out of mind in a corner of the attic where it stayed for who knows how long and never bothered a soul. But people don't stop to think that those old guns were usually kept loaded. It took a while to load them, so they were hung ready for instant use when they were needed.

After all that time, when the kid pulled the trigger, he didn't have to holler "bang!" The gun spoke louder than he, and now he must live with the consequences for the rest of his life.

Yes, you need to understand enough about old guns to fulfill your police role as protector.

4.1 The First Gun

The ancestor of all firearms is the hand cannon. It appeared during the fourteenth century and by the end of that century it was known throughout Europe. It was simply a barrel, closed at the back end, and attached to a wooden handle. It was loaded from the muzzle and fired by touching a burning match to the touch hole at the breech end.

The principle has remained the same throughout history, but we do it much more conveniently and efficiently now.

4.2 Early Gun Locks

Because it was difficult for nervous hands to hold a burning match to a tiny hole, the first improvement in guns appeared about 1450, the matchlock. It was nothing more than a lever that precisely positioned the burning match to the touch hole when the trigger was pulled.

The wheel lock was developed about the same time as the matchlock and proved to be the better. A serrated wheel was wound up against a spring. A piece of iron pyrite was held by a lever so it contacted the spinning wheel when the trigger was pulled. Sort of like a cigarette lighter.

To avoid the special tool needed to wind up the wheel lock's spring, the snaphance was developed. The hammer clamped onto a piece of iron pyrite. When the trigger was pulled, this "flint" struck a glancing blow against an anvil to shower sparks down into an open pan. This lock reigned supreme for some 80 years.

The flintlock improved upon the open pan idea, in about 1615. The priming pan was covered with a hinged lid, and an ear called the "frizzen" took the place of the anvil. When the hammer fell, it hit the frizzen and pushed it up enough to let the sparks enter the pan.

The advent of the percussion cap system in 1814 greatly simplified gun locks. A nipple replaced the touch hole. The cap fitted on the nipple. As in modern ignition systems, the hammer struck the cap and fired its spark through the hole into the powder charge. Because the hole was covered, you'd be surprised how long a loaded percussion gun can remain "hot" when stored under dry conditions.

The flintlock is what you see in all the old pirate pictures. This British Navy Pistol is .50 caliber, and may have seen service fighting buccaneers. Note Tower of London stamp at left of sideplate.

A familiar example of the percussion revolver is the Remington "cap and ball." It helped to tame the wild frontier before Sam Colt made his famous Peacemaker.

This percussion muzzle-loading shotgun may have hung over the mantle in some frontier cabin. You find replicas of modern manufacture being used in competition and for fun.

4.3 Making Old Guns Safe

You can encounter flintlock or percussion lock guns even today. Antiques are still popular for decorative purposes. Replicas are being manufactured for the sport of muzzleloader target shooting and hunting. Clubs hold muzzle-loading matches, and some states have separate hunting seasons restricted to muzzleloaders.

To fully unload a muzzleloader without firing it literally requires a special tool to auger into the ball and pull it out.

To make the flintlock safe, without such a tool, open the pan and make sure the pan is empty.

To render the percussion gun safe, cock the hammer and remove the copper-colored percussion cap from the nipple.

Then let the hammer down, easy.

4.4 Damascus: Dangerous to Shoot

Granddad's old shotgun hung over the mantle for many years and it was a beautiful gun to see. Its barrel seemed to be etched with a spiral design. Gramps had always taken the best care of that gun. But now it could be a death trap.

Damascus steel was once highly desired for sword blades, and many old guns were made with Damascus barrels. Confidence in this type of steel was once so great that cheap gun barrels were sometimes painted or etched with acid to give them the appearance of true Damascus.

Damascus barrels were made by braiding strips of iron and steel and tightly twisting this braid around a mandrel. Through a welding process with repeated light hammering, the twisted braid was joined into a solid mass. The mandrel was then bored out and the barrel polished inside and out. Cheap Damascus barrels containing mostly iron were often hastily produced to meet a low price. Since they are actually a continuous mass of welds, only the greatest care and skill turned out a good barrel.

Today's modern smokeless powders develop higher pressures than the old black powder for which these barrels originally were made. One imperfect weld in a Damascus barrel — most were of medium or low grade — creates a weak spot that could let go when the next shot was fired. When it did explode, it usually was right at the point where the shooter's hand holds the fore-end of the gun.

Modern open-hearth steel, at its worst, is better than the best Damascus. So, if you have a family heirloom, a beautiful old gun handed down for generations, examine it closely. Should the barrel have this watered, spiral look, take it to a good gunsmith. Have him alter it so it can't be fired, or lock it in a glass case for permanent display, *not* for shooting.

5

Form Follows Function

Your shotgun is most likely a 12-gauge pump with an 18- or 20-inch barrel. It probably has a regular wood stock, but it may have a folding stock, or just a pistol grip. It may have a bead front sight on a shot barrel or rifle sights on a slug barrel. The gun can be configured virtually any way you want it. These options may be available on guns from the factory, or you can change parts on existing guns with aftermarket accessories.

There could be 147 different configurations of the shotgun you are issued. So what's right for you?

The man who writes specifications for gun purchases for your department may be your firearms instructor. As you develop preferences or dislikes for particular features, discuss them with him. If he knows what you want, and don't want, it could influence the next invitation to bid. But you won't get far if you want a $300 auto to replace your $150 pump. That's one reason you see more pump guns in police cruisers.

The pump type of gun action requires that you operate the fore-end manually by moving it fully to the rear after firing to eject the empty shell and cock the hammer, then by pushing it forward to chamber a new round ready to fire again. The auto, or self-loading, action does this for you *automatically* using the recoil or gas pressure generated from firing the shell. It's really semi-automatic because you have to pull the trigger for every shot. But that's too

29

Browning BPS.

long a word so everyone calls them "autos." Then there's the familiar hinged break-action with a lever on top that you push sideways to open.

For years, the old line gunmakers have offered police models of their popular and proven sporting shotguns. Nowadays you see guns specifically designed for law enforcement use. Here's a selection of what we find on the market today, categorized by action type and listed alphabetically by brand name.

5.1 Pump Action Shotguns

5.1.1 Browning

Manufactured by Browning, the BPS features bottom loading and ejecting. There's no ejection port in the side. With a top tang safety, this gun is equally convenient for right- or left-handed shooters. It has double action bars and is offered with an 18½-inch bead sight or a 20-inch rifle sight barrel. Its receiver is forged and machined from solid bar stock. Barrels are chambered for 3-inch shells.

5.1.2 Ithaca

Manufactured by the Ithaca Gun Co., this time-honored John M. Browning–designed shotgun dates back to 1937 — thus, the Model 37. It is distinct from other pump-action shotgun designs.

Ithaca Model 37 M&P 8-shot pump-action.

Ithaca Model 37 M&P 5-shot pump-action.

An obvious difference is the solid-sided receiver. Loading and ejecting are done through one common opening in the bottom of the receiver. This is an advantage in making the gun equally convenient for right- or left-handed shooters. It's a disadvantage if the shooter induces an ejection malfunction by short-stroking the action. The resultant jam is not easily cleared.

Another difference is the absence of a disconnector. In a rapid fire situation, you can hold back the trigger and fire successive shots simply by cycling the action.

Military and Police (M&P) versions of the 12-gauge Model 37 are offered in five-shot models with 18½- or 20-inch barrels, Parkerized finish; or eight-shot models with 20-inch barrels, Parkerized or matte chrome finish. These guns are also offered with wood stock or handgrip.

The Deerslayer model comes with a 20-inch rifle-sighted barrel that is bored slightly tighter than straight cylinder bore for improved accuracy with rifled slugs.

5.1.3 Mossberg

Manufactured by O. F. Mossberg & Sons, the Model 500 Security pump-action shotgun is offered in six-shot, 18½-inch barrel or eight-shot, 20-inch barrel versions, both cylinder bore. It is available in 12- or 20-gauge, or .410-bore with the option of rifle sights or bead front sights; blue, nickel, or Parkerized finish. The safety is top tang-mounted. Weight of the 12-gauge gun is seven pounds.

Mossberg Model 500 Security pump-action.

New Mossberg Bullpup.

The Cruiser Persuader shotgun is the Model 500 fitted with the "cruiser" pistol grip and a folding stock. The muzzle is machined with "muzzle brake" slots to help reduce recoil. Weight is held to 5¾ pounds and overall length to 28 inches with the 18½-inch barrel.

There's a new Bullpup version of the venerable Model 500. Using high-impact, molded materials, Mossberg now has a compact, user-oriented gun that can take what you dish out. Specifications and availability were not available at this writing, but it will come with an 18½- or 20-inch barrel in 12-gauge only.

The idea of the Bullpup is to set the metal parts farther to the rear than in a standard gun. The ejection port of the receiver is about halfway between your shoulder and firing hand.

The Model 3000, produced by Howa of Japan, gained a reputation as being the best police shotgun on the market when it was branded "Smith & Wesson." With S&W's divestiture, Mossberg quickly grabbed the long gun line. They also bought S&W's inventory in the process, so you may still see some guns with the old brand name—if they haven't all become collector's items, stashed away in gun cabinets.

The Model 3000 Police Shotgun is in the Mossberg line, but not quite in the 147 flavors offered by S&W. Basic variations include 18- or 20-inch barrels. Choate stocks, folding stocks, pistol grips, and magazine tube extensions are made to fit this gun, so you should have no trouble getting it configured the way you want it.

The Model 3000 has double action bars. The magazine tube and ejector are installed with epoxy, so your armorer can replace them. The 12-gauge, 2¾-inch chamber barrel is made of chrome molybdenum steel. The cross-bolt safety is reversible for right- or left-handed operation.

5.1.4 Remington

Manufactured by Remington Arms–du Pont, the Remington 870P pump—for more than thirty years—has been the staple of the police arsenal.

Remington Model 870 Police Shotgun; pump-action, 12-gauge only.

Remington Model 870 shown with folding stock, pistol grip, and magazine tube extension.

This is the police version of the popular sporting shotgun, of which more than four million have been manufactured since 1950. It features a receiver machined from a solid block of steel and double action bars.

The Model 870P is offered with a choice of finishes, blue or Parkerized, and optional accessories. The gun can be ordered with a varnish or oil finish wood stock, or a folding stock. Magazine tube extensions increase shell capacity to seven or eight shots. The seven-shot extension is used with the 18-inch barrel. Either seven- or eight-shot extensions can be used with the 20-inch barrel. A variety of sling swivels are offered to suit various configurations.

Barrel choices are 20-inch, rifle sight, improved cylinder; 20-inch, bead sight, cylinder bore; or 18-inch, bead sight, cylinder bore.

With a wood stock and 20-inch barrel, the Remington 870P weighs about 6¾ pounds; overall length is 40½ inches; stock length with recoil pad is 14 inches; drop at heel is 2½ inches; drop at comb is 1⅝ inches. With a folding stock, weight is about seven pounds 11 ounces; overall length, with the stock folded, is only 30½ inches with the 20-inch barrel.

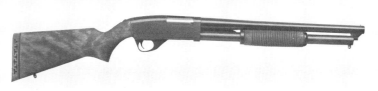

Savage Model 69-RXL Pump-Action Riot Gun; 7-shot.

5.1.5 Savage

Manufactured by Savage Industries, the Model 69-RXL is a compact, fast-shooting pump-action shotgun designed with security in mind. It offers seven-shot capacity with one in the chamber when using 2¾-inch shells. It has an oil-rubbed hardwood stock and fore-end, and a three-inch chamber.

The safety is located on the top tang, convenient for both right- and left-handed persons. The trigger and sear are both inoperable when the safety button is in the rear "safe" position.

5.1.6 Winchester

Manufactured by U.S. Repeating Arms Co., the familiar Winchester brand shotguns are manufactured by USRA in the original New Haven, Connecticut factory, with a lot of new machinery. There are three Security pump-action shotguns offered, all with 18-inch cylinder bore barrels and twin action bars. One pin receiver group disassembly makes cleaning easy. The Defender has a low-glare blue finish and an eight-shot capacity magazine. The Stainless Marine and Police models have stainless steel barrels, triple-plated chrome finish and a seven-shot capacity.

The Defender is available in either 12- or 20-gauge. The Stainless Police comes in 12-gauge only, with either bead sight or rifle-type front and rear sights.

The guns with triple-plated finishes are first plated with copper for adher-

Winchester Stainless Police, pump-action.

Winchester Defender, shown with pistol grip; pump-action.

H&K Benelli Model 121 M1 pump-action.

ence, then with nickel for rust protection, and finally with chrome for a hard finish.

All three guns are available with a pistol grip of ABS plastic, rather than a full butt stock.

5.2 Autoloading Shotguns

5.2.1 Benelli

Imported by Heckler & Koch, the Benelli 121 M1 semi-automatic defense shotgun has a unique inertia-locking bolt system that "minimizes recoil and maximizes accuracy," according to the company.

"I was able to hand-throw eight clay targets holding the shotgun in one hand and throwing the targets with the other and break each one of them in a video-documented time of 1.77 seconds," says International Skeet Champion John Satterwhite. "It's a popular gun in European shotgun matches, especially in England."

The gun is an eight-shot, short recoil-operated action with fixed front and rear sights for rifled slug adaptability. It weighs slightly more than seven pounds and is less than 41 inches in overall length, with a 20-inch cylinder bore barrel.

The 121 M1's days are probably numbered, however, by the new "star" of H&K's police shotguns: a new Benelli shotgun designed specifically for law enforcement officers. Details were not available at press time.

The new Benelli M1 Super 90 is so named because "it is a gun designed for

New H&K Benelli.

the '90s." It's so new, in fact, that the photo is of the first prototype to come into the country, which has a rotating locking lug system on the bolt, fewer parts in the bolt than the old-style Benelli, and a new shell release system.

The shell release functions to feed one shell from the magazine tube onto the carrier, so you don't have to feed the first shell into the chamber. If you carry most autos with the chamber empty and magazine loaded, the bolt will lock back when you pull the charging handle. Then you have to press a release to close the bolt. With this new Benelli M1 Super 90, touching the shell release puts a shell on the carrier; jack the action and you're in business.

For safety's sake, you can remove the shell from the chamber without releasing another from the magazine. Put that shell back into the chamber and the gun's fully loaded again.

The carrier is "free." You don't have to press a release button to load the magazine. Once the bolt closes on a chambered shell, you can add shells to the magazine as you do with a pump gun.

This new Benelli M1 Super 90 features a one-piece, alloy receiver, unbreakable forearm and pistol grip stock with recoil pad, black non-glare finish, eight-shot capacity, and a new patridge rear sight adjustable for windage. Total gun weight is about seven pounds.

5.2.2 Ithaca

On the high end of the scale, Ithaca offers the "Mag-10 Roadblocker," a semi-automatic 10-gauge Magnum that is said to be able to stop a car. It delivers half again the power and shot weight of a 12-gauge. Felt recoil is comparable to that of a 12 because of Ithaca's Countercoil™ gas system.

5.2.3 Sage International

The Model SW Sidewinder is a modified Remington Model 1100 auto-loading shotgun. The action spring is relocated from the butt stock, so that a folding or telescoping stock can be fitted. The gun's inherently low recoil is further reduced by Pro-Port™ barrel venting.

Ithaca Mag-10 Roadblocker, pump-action.

STEVENS
Model 311-R
Double Barrel Guard Gun

Stevens Model 311-R Guard Gun; double barrel.

The Model SW1 is equipped with a 22-inch rifle sighted barrel and has a nine-shot capacity. SW2 has a 20-inch plain barrel and eight-shot capacity; the SW3 has an 18-inch barrel and seven-shot capacity. All are available with either a telescoping stock or side-folding stock.

The Model SW-PC is equipped with a pistol grip and 14½-inch barrel for an overall length of 24½ inches, and a capacity of four shells in the magazine and one in the chamber.

5.3 Break Action Shotguns

Doc Holliday's double-barrel Greener opened by hinging the barrels to "break" them open from the receiver. Many "sawed-off" shotguns today are made from double- or even single-barrel guns using this type of action.

5.3.1 Stevens

Savage Industries makes the Fox and Stevens brands of double guns and the Stevens Model 311-R, 12-gauge Security Double comes with 18¼-inch barrels, both cylinder bore. It has double triggers, one for each barrel, and an oil-finished hardwood butt stock with full pistol grip and rubber recoil pad. The top tang safety goes "on" automatically when you open the action. It will take three-inch Magnum shells and weighs 6¾ pounds.

5.4 Special Shotguns

5.4.1 Franchi

Imported by F. I. E. Corp., the Franchi SPAS 12, manufactured in Brescia, Italy, is either a pump-action or gas-operated semi-automatic shotgun, selectable as you choose.

"A self-loader functions fine with the more powerful high brass shells," says FIE's Ron Vogel. "But you may need to use low pressure loads and the

Franchi SPAS 12.

SPAS handles them in the pump action mode. If an autoloader jams it can be difficult to clear. Switch to pump action and you can clear it."

Vogel says the U.S. Coast Guard is evaluating the SPAS 12 for adoption as the gun it uses when boarding vessels at sea.

Chambered for 2¾-inch shells it claims a nine-shot capacity, eight in the magazine and one in the chamber. The gun weighs 9.6 pounds. It has a Parkerized finish, alloy receiver, chrome-lined steel barrel, folding stock, nylon/resin pistol grip and fore-end. The 21½-inch barrel is cylinder bore but optional full or modified screw-on choke tubes are available. Overall length is 31¾ inches with stock folded, 41 inches with it extended.

5.4.2 Ithaca

Responding to specialized needs of the police market, Ithaca offers the "Stakeout." This new 20-gauge pump is claimed to be the "world's lightest, most concealable shotgun." With a five-shot magazine, handgrip, and 13¼-inch barrel, the Stakeout weighs only 3½ pounds.

The 20-gauge is plenty adequate for use in undercover situations, and it's certainly more comfortable to shoot then a 12 in this "chopped down" configuration. This model is also offered in 12-gauge, Parkerized or matte chrome

Ithaca Model 37 Stakeout – 20 gauge

Ithaca Model 37 Stakeout; 20-gauge.

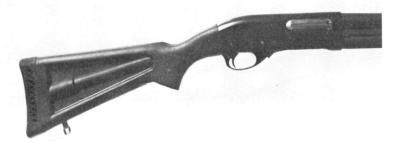

Choate butt stock replacement.

finish, if you're a glutton for punishment. Since it falls under the definition of a "firearm" under federal law, it's available only to police.

5.5 Accessories

There's a variety of products from many manufacturers aimed at adding convenience or responding to special needs of law enforcement. What follows is far from complete. It simply illustrates the kinds of accessories offered.

5.5.1 Choate Machine & Tool

You'll find that many of the options offered on factory-new shotguns are manufactured by Choate.

It's easier and more economical to buy the guns originally specified with the accessories you want. But if your old wooden butt stock looks like it survived the Indian Wars, you can replace it with an almost indestructible fiberglass-filled plastic stock that is six to eight times stronger than wood. The same material is used to make a pistol grip stock that enables easier one-hand firing of the shotgun. You can replace the stock with just a pistol grip and add a top-folding or side-folding stock, if you wish. If your guns have a standard magazine, you can increase their capacity with a choice of two magazine tube extensions for 18- or 20-inch barrels.

These are all aftermarket accessories offered by Choate.

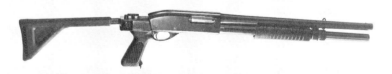

Choate side-swinging folding stock, with pistol grip.

Choate pistol-grip stock.

5.5.2 Hi-Caliber Products

The Ammo Glove is a black ballistic nylon sheath that fits over the stock and is held in place by Velcro®. It holds five extra shells, two facing one way and three the other.

5.5.3 Michaels of Oregon

This company offers a variety of leather and nylon slings for police rifles and shotguns. Universal Quick Detachable swivel sets are made for all popular brands of guns.

5.5.4 Sage International

The company's Model TS870 telescoping stock replaces the wood butt stock on the Remington 870 or Smith & Wesson 3000. Quick open features enable the butt pad to be flipped down and pulled rearward for stock extension. A button must be depressed to release the stock for storage. Support rails are round.

5.5.5 Sound-Off Safety

Made by Kleis Leather Products, the "Flap" cartridge case is a Cordura® nylon ammo holder that stays with the gun and protects the ammo it holds. An elastic strap goes around the butt to prevent slipping, and it fastens snugly with Velcro straps. The flap is closed at the top with Velcro so shotshells are protected from the elements; even so, you can get to them quickly. It's available in black or camouflage, right- or left-handed, 12- or 20-gauge shotshells or .30 caliber cartridges.

5.5.6 Special Weapons Products

Its Ammo Carrier, Model 1430, holds seven extra shells on the right side of the butt stock in a pocket with a Velcro flap that opens at the bottom. There's an exterior loop at the bottom that holds one shell for a quick reload. During tests at the Chapman Academy, it earned high marks.

6

Fodder Takes Many Forms

What good is your patrol car without gasoline? Or a computer without software? Likewise, your gun is only a bunch of metal parts until you mate it with the expendable items it uses to perform its function. Your gun is only the tool that fires the ammunition you feed it.

6.1 History

The Chinese are credited with inventing the stuff that explodes inside the firecracker. Legend has it that knowledge of this mixture of materials made its way through the Near East to Europe. We know that Friar Roger Bacon (1214–1294) was the first European to record it. Bacon's mixture of sulphur, saltpeter, and charcoal powders brought a flash of fire when ignited with a hot coal. But, being powder, it absorbed moisture easily and formed lumps that burned more slowly.

By the mid-sixteenth century, a little water was added to the mixture and it was extruded into small pellets. When dried, these pellets burned more uniformly. Essentially, that's how gunpowder is made today.

A Scottish clergyman—Alexander John Forsyth—developed the use of fulminates as priming mixtures. These are salts produced by dissolving metals in acid. When struck a hard blow, these salts explode with a flash. Fulminate of mercury is the priming mix used today.

Forsyth's invention enabled the development of percussion lock guns. It also led to the first breechloader. Packaging pre-measured portions of powder and shot in a combustible container formed the paper cartridge; but the primer was still a separate percussion cap.

The first center-fire shotgun shell was developed by a Frenchman, Samuel Pauly. He devised a paper body shell with a brass head and, for the first time, a primer was positioned in the center of the head. While his system is similar to modern ammunition, Pauly was 50 years ahead of his time. His shell and break-open breech gun were not entirely dependable, so were never widely used. But his concept set the stage for the development of shotshells.

A variety of self-contained cartridge designs came and went. Priming compound was put in a teat, under a pin, or inside a crushable rim, and finally into a separate little cup that was held in a receptacle formed in the brass base of the shell. Powder was measured into the shell and covered with a wad. The shot charge was poured in and the open end was crimped over a top wad card to close it. Modern shells are closed with a folded crimp rather than a top card wad, which disrupts the shot column, and present-day manufacturers use a variety of devices and materials to protect the shot as it travels through the barrel.

6.2 Ammunition Parts

The preceding paragraphs highlight what others have spent volumes to explain, but we now know that a shotshell consists of five parts: the case, primer, powder, wads, and shot. There are different types of powders for different types of shotshells. But the manufacturers take care of that choice. What more do we need to know?

Only that modern smokeless powder does not explode. It burns. Rapidly, to be sure. Pull the bullet out of a .22 cartridge and spill its powder into an ashtray. Touch a match to it and it only burns, no bang. What makes it powerful is that the product of burning is a lot of gas that has to go somewhere. If it is contained in your stomach, you know where it goes. If it is constrained inside the shell in the chamber of a firearm, it's going to push through the path of least resistance — the shot charge moves before anything else. The rapidly expanding gases push it through the bore and send it on its way.

6.3 Gauge

Metallic cartridges and the guns for them are sized by "caliber," the measure of the bore or bullet diameter in inches. Metric measure is in millimeters. But "gauge" is ancient in origin and is something else. If the bore of your gun fits a round lead ball and it takes 12 of those balls to make one pound, yours is

A typical shotshell is shown in this cutaway drawing. *1.* Folded crimp. *2.* Shot enclosed in plastic cup. *3.* Tube. *4.* Plastic wad column. *5.* Smokeless powder. *6.* Metal head. *7.* Base wad. *8.* Primer. *Federal Cartridge Corp.*

a 12-gauge gun. If it takes 20 balls to make a pound, it's a 20-gauge. And so on.

The .410, however, is an American development and it's really a caliber. The bore of a .410 has an inside diameter of .410 inches. So call it a .410-bore and you'll sound like an expert.

6.4 Shot vs. Slug

Shot ranges in size from a #9 pellet measuring .08 inches to the massive 000 Buck .36 inches. That's .36 caliber, actually as big as the bullet from your handgun. A bird hunter uses the smaller size shot because he doesn't want a lot of penetration, yet he wants the shock effect of multiple pellets. One ounce of #9 shot counts 600 pellets. A hunter who goes after larger game uses buck shot because he needs the added penetration to reach vital organs deep inside the animal. A standard velocity 00 Buck shell will nominally contain nine pellets, each the size of a .33 caliber ball.

The rifled slug shell virtually turns your shotgun into a rifle, out to about 100 yards with a fair degree of accuracy. Its one-ounce slug is awesome.

We cut a slug shell open to show the rifled slug. A whole shell shows the top of the slug inside.

Slugs penetrate deeply. An aggressor behind a brick wall, for example, isn't safe. Even several apartment walls fail to stop a rifled slug from a shotgun. How often do you expect to need such slugs? Actually, it's worth having a couple with you in the rare case you may have to make a long shot, or punch through an assailant's cover. SWAT carries rifles for those purposes, but the slug shell can turn your shotgun into a rifle.

00 Buck can do virtually everything the patrol officer needs to do, unless it's a situation that clearly calls for a rifle. You should be familiar with how your gun shoots with slug loads, just for those rare situations where you need them. You can swap shells quickly to take out a terrorist hiding behind a car door.

6.5 Shot Loads

Shot loads most used in police work are "buck shot" and the most popular size is 00 Buck.

00 Buck translates to .33 caliber and a standard shell holds nine pellets. A Magnum shell has 12. That's one shot throwing more lead than you can produce by emptying your revolver *twice*.

Each pellet of #4 Buck is .24 caliber, and a standard shell contains 27. The

Magnum #4 Buck load has 41 pellets. Sounds devastating. But the lighter pellets lack penetration. They don't have the effective range of 00 Buck.

I've heard arguments favoring both sizes, but a consensus seems to be that the 00 Buck will do everything the policeman needs it to do. The heavier 00 pellet will have better individual penetration. Remember, the shotgun is an "offensive" weapon.

6.6 Ammunition Makers

6.6.1 Federal Cartridge Corp.

Federal Premium™ brand buckshot loads use an extra-hard, copper-plated pellet protected by a granulated buffer material. The company claims a unique method of layering pellets in the shell for additional protection.

Premium loads are offered in 00 Buck with 9 pellets, and Magnum with a dozen 00 Buck, or 34 #4 Buck.

Hi-Power™ brand buckshot loads are offered in the full range from #4 to 000 in 12-gauge, and 00 or #4 Buck in 10-gauge.

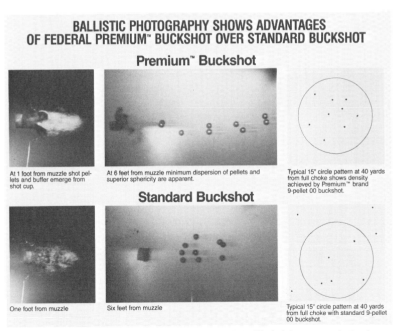

BALLISTIC PHOTOGRAPHY SHOWS ADVANTAGES OF FEDERAL PREMIUM™ BUCKSHOT OVER STANDARD BUCKSHOT

Premium™ Buckshot

At 1 foot from muzzle shot pellets and buffer emerge from shot cup.

At 6 feet from muzzle minimum dispersion of pellets and superior sphericity are apparent.

Typical 15" circle pattern at 40 yards from full choke shows density achieved by Premium™ brand 9-pellet 00 buckshot.

Standard Buckshot

One foot from muzzle

Six feet from muzzle

Typical 15" circle pattern at 40 yards from full choke with standard 9-pellet 00 buckshot.

There can be differences in shot shell loads, as this ballistic laboratory photo shows. *Federal Cartridge Corp.*

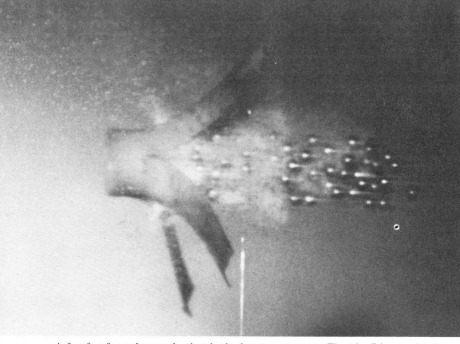

A few feet from the muzzle, the plastic shot cup opens up. The "dust" is granulated plastic shot buffer. The shot column continues in a tight bunch. *Federal Cartridge Corp.*

Federal offers a heavier-than-usual 1¼-ounce hollow-point rifled slug load in 12-gauge Magnum with a stated muzzle energy of 2,695 ft. lbs. A standard one-ounce 12-gauge slug load and a 10-gauge Magnum with a ¾-ounce rifled slug are also offered.

6.6.2 Remington

Remington loads a full range of shotshells. Of prime interest to law enforcement officers are buckshot loads from #4 to 000. Traditionally the more popular in America are the 3¾ dram equivalent standard loads in 00 Buck with nine pellets .33 inches in diameter, and the #4 Buck with 27 pellets .24 inches in diameter. Magnum buckshot loads offer 12 pellets in 00 Buck, or 20 pellets in 1 Buck, both with more than 4 drams equivalent powder charges.

The Slugger rifled slug load offers a one-ounce slug at a muzzle velocity of 1,560 fps and 2,364 ft. lbs. muzzle energy.

Dummy training rounds are also available.

6.6.3 Winchester-Olin

This year, Winchester introduced new Double-X buckshot loads. The 2¾-inch 00 Buck carries 9 pellets, the 2¾-inch Magnum 12 pellets, and the

3-inch Magnum 15 pellets. The Double-X shell uses copper-plated lead shot in Super Grex™ buffering material, which is claimed to protect the shot for tighter patterns and greater effective range.

Winchester also loads 00 Buck in a 9 pellet standard load, and a 12 pellet Magnum load.

The Super-X hollow-point rifled slug load, in 12-gauge, has a one-ounce slug at a muzzle velocity of 1,600 fps.

6.6.4 *Ballistic Research Industries*

BRI loads a variety of special purpose shells.

The Gualandi Slug features "unibody" construction. There's an integral base wad for stability, and there's a conical nose for efficient air flow for better accuracy and extended range.

BRI's Sabot Bullet is a wasp-waist .50 caliber bullet in a sabot. When fired, the sabot splits and drops away. At the second annual Shotgun Slug World Championship, these Sabot 500's placed first, second, and third in benchrest competition; second and third in the offhand match.

6.6.5 *North American Ordnance*

The Elast-A-Slug is designed for situations where crowd restraint is needed without lethal force. It is suggested as an alternative to tear gas, when use of chemical agent is inappropriate.

Because direct impact with an Elast-A-Slug can be lethal up to 30 yards, these cartridges are intended to be fired against the surface about two-thirds of the distance to the target. Low-angle deflection ricochets the 145-grain slug into the target. Used in this manner, effective range is stated by the manufacturer as 3 to 45 yards. Velocity of the Elast-A-Slug is 800 to 850 fps.

7

Loading the Shotgun

Suppose you've fired several rounds and must still cover a potential threat. Can you stuff more rounds into the magazine while maintaining target acquisition?

Suppose you've fired the shotgun dry. You'd be better off with a baseball bat — unless you know how to get two more rounds into that gun in under two seconds, while keeping your attention on the target.

In either case, could you fire while reloading? Of course you could, and possibly save your life. Even the Indians knew enough to attack while their adversary was reloading.

7.1 Car Carry Condition

If you had to draw a shotgun at the beginning of your shift, load it and lock it in the rack in the cruiser, you weren't concerned about speed. If the shotgun is left in the rack without handling between shifts, it's likely the magazine is loaded and the action is closed on an empty chamber. There are more than a few cruisers with holes in their roofs because the gun was closed on a *loaded* chamber and the safety wasn't "on."

Accordingly, it's best that you check to make sure the chamber is empty, close the action, and put the safety "on." Then slip the shells into the magazine tube to its full capacity. The gun may be left cocked.

7.2 Action Release

In a shotgun instructor class I attended we loaded our guns in this "car condition carry." On the command "fire," more than half the class couldn't rack a round into the chamber. Yes, I was among those who forgot. You might just push the safety off, then fumble because the action won't open to feed a shell into the chamber. Remember, the action is locked when it's closed and the gun is cocked.

You've got to release the action to open it when the gun is cocked. And you'd better have that idea ingrained into your brain if you need that shotgun in a hurry.

Reach around the front of the trigger guard and press the slide release. Then as you mount the gun, your finger comes right back to the trigger. This sequence provides economy of motion and time.

But suppose you've fired a few shots and there are still adversaries threatening you?

You're holding the shotgun pointed in the general direction of the threat — in the ready position. Your right hand grips the weapon at the small of the stock. The butt is tucked between your forearm and your body. Your left hand is on the fore-end. Let go with your left hand.

Surprised? You can still hold the shotgun and keep your eyes on the threat. You could shoot the gun this way, if you had to. While you pay attention to the threat area, your left hand grabs more shells from your belt or

There are many types of cruiser gunlocks. East Windsor (Conn.) Officer Stephen Andrusko prefers the *muzzle-down-type* in his car.

pocket. Even if you take these shells from your pocket one at a time, with practice, you can have the gun fully loaded in something like five or six seconds.

7.3 Combat Loading

Suppose you're in a fire fight and those four shells in the magazine tube went quickly. You've wrung the gun dry and there are still adversaries threatening you? It would be nice to have a fully loaded gun. But if the situation is still hot, you need to get whatever shells you can into the gun *immediately*. You are more proficient with your strong hand, so use it.

7.3.1 Loading Position

We'll be talking later about the ready position: gun in front of you with the front bead on the target and the butt stock level with your forearm. From the ready, open the action. That's the "loading" position. You can easily hold the gun with your weak hand on the fore-end and reach for two extra shells with your strong hand.

7.3.2 Loading Two Shells

It works fastest if you have two shells base-up in that neat little carrier on your belt. But it can work from the pocket. The heavy end of the shell is the

If the gun is cocked, you have to push the action release before the action will open. On this gun, it's at the front of the trigger guard.

Combat loading means you need two shells where you can get them *fast*. This Rogers two-shell carrier fits a duty belt.

Drop the bottom shell in through the ejection port and close the action . . .

then roll the other shell to the underside and slip it into the magazine tube.

When you have time, you can add more shells to the magazine with the off-hand.

shot end. Even in your pocket, they tend to ride shot-end down. You can feel the rim; so, by touch, you can grab two shells from your pocket with the shot-end forward.

The recommended grasp is with your middle finger between the two, index finger on top, and third finger at the bottom, all pressing against your thumb. Try grabbing and holding two shells that way with your strong hand. Easy, huh?

With two shells in your fingers, drop the bottom one into the ejection port. Quickly close the action with the weak hand. You could fire the gun now, if you had to. Roll the remaining shell around the receiver and push it into the magazine tube with your thumb. Now you've got two shells in the gun and you'd be surprised how quickly you can do it.

7.3.3 It's Faster with Practice

In that shotgun instructor course, instructors Jerry Lane and Bill Burroughs put us through this combat loading exercise. At first, it took anywhere from four to six seconds. Before the week was out, everyone in the class was combat-loading two shells in less than three seconds. One guy even did it in under two seconds.

Jerry Lane is left-handed. Lefties load always with the right hand. He drops the bottom shell into the ejection port. . .

7.3.4 *Adding More Shells*

When you have time, you can finish stuffing more shells into the maga-zine with the weak hand. Hold the gun with the strong hand, pointed in the direction of a potential threat, and insert additional rounds into the magazine with the weak hand. All this time you can watch the target and react with a shot, if necessary.

7.3.5 *Left-Handed Mode*

The procedure is a little different for left-handers. Because it's a right-handed world and the ejection port is on the right side of the gun, lefties should load all shells with their right hand. Holding the pistol grip with your strong left hand, drop one shell into the ejection port and push the fore-end forward with the heel of your right hand. The second shell is rolled around the receiver and slipped into the magazine tube. Then, as time allows, stuff addi-tional shells into the magazine with your right hand.

7.4 Unloading the Shotgun

The shotgun should be unloaded and action left open before cleaning or passing it to another person on the range; or the situation on the street has eased and the sergeant doesn't want combat-ready shotguns waving around.

then he closes the action by pushing the fore-end forward with his right hand . . .

and finally pushes the second shell into the magazine with his right hand.

Unloading a shotgun like a professional is easy. Open the action slowly and catch the ejecting shell. . .

jiggle the gun so the shell on the carrier drops out and you have two in the hand.

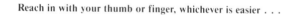

Reach in with your thumb or finger, whichever is easier . . .

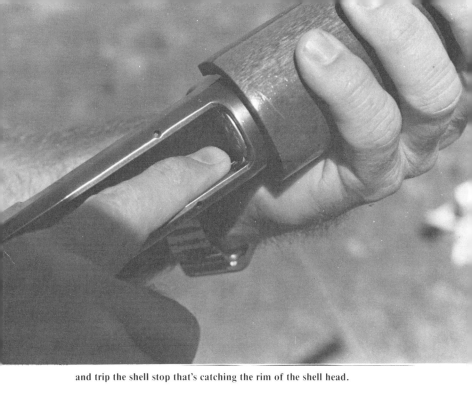

and trip the shell stop that's catching the rim of the shell head.

The released shell will drop out into your hand. Repeat until the magazine is empty.

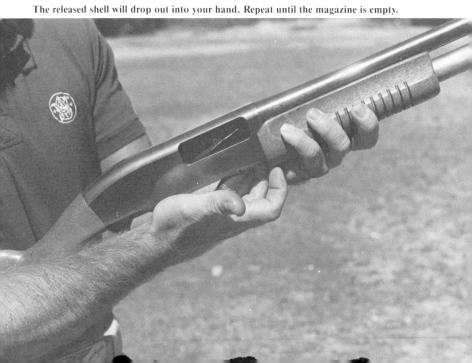

How many times have you seen someone hold the action release and shuck successive shells onto the ground? This not only looks unprofessional in front of the public, but you may have to stake your life on one of those shells that was summarily bounced off the concrete.

Unloading is most professionally done by opening the action slowly, catching the ejected shell in your right hand, and dumping out the shell on the carrier at the same time. While leaving the action open, push the carrier up from the bottom. Then trip the shell stop with your finger. In this way, you can pop shells from the magazine tube one-by-one right into your hand.

Some shotguns have two shell stops. One works when the action is open, the other when the action is closed. The one you want is on the left on an S&W Model 3000 and Mossberg 500, and on the right side of a Remington 870. You want the one that releases the shells with the action open for the S&W and Remington shotguns. On the Mossberg, empty the mag tube with the action closed. Then there's the Ithaca 37; the only way to unload its magazine tube is to shuck the shells out one at a time.

This unloading technique makes you look like you know what you're doing. It looks professional to the public and it protects those unfired shells.

8

Carrying the Shotgun

Unless you're a hunter accustomed to carrying a loaded shotgun around all day, the times that you have the gun in hand are usually under stress. On shotgun qualification day you may practice shucking a few shells through the pump gun at a cardboard target, and observe a demonstration of how to load and unload the gun.

But you're probably not practiced in handling the shotgun *off* the firing range.

The hunter develops habits that make his gun safe until a bird flushes. The policeman searching with a shotgun in hand is doing the same thing as the hunter, so the same rules apply.

- Never point your gun at anything you don't want to shoot.
- Keep the safety on until you are ready to fire.

Keep the gun pointed in a safe direction, for it's quite disconcerting to see that big 12-gauge hole looking your way. When the situation is at ease, there's no gun safer than one with the action open. It takes only a second to close it, when you need it.

8.1 Situation at Ease

If there is no immediate threat, it makes no sense to arm a time-bomb. You wouldn't cock your pistol, would you? You don't pull the pin on a grenade until you're ready to throw it. So why carry the shotgun with a shell under the firing pin?

The safest carry is with the magazine and chamber empty and action open with the safety "on." That's how the gun should be when you are handling it in the classroom, or on the range, and there's no chance of threat.

Remember, the safety is a mechanical device subject to wear and failure. It should *never* be the sole basis for safety.

When carrying the shotgun, the officer should employ the same safety precautions as the sportsman. The hunter's carries are good.

- *Carry Condition One:* Crook the gun over your strong arm, butt under your armpit, muzzle down and in front where you can see it.
- *Carry Condition Two:* Crook the gun over your weak side arm, hand covering the trigger guard, muzzle up but to the side where you can't see it.

In both carries, the magazine tube may be loaded, but the action is open and the safety is on, with a shell resting on the shell carrier. If you were to roll the gun to the right, that shell would drop out of the ejection port. But you can see how quickly you could be ready to shoot.

If you are in a situation of potential threat, you must be able to get that gun ready in a hurry. It's a personal preference of mine to carry the shotgun with the magazine loaded but the action closed and *uncocked* on an empty chamber. The gun won't go off accidentally. There's no way it could fire without your taking positive and definite action — first.

Racking the action to load the chamber takes little time. While it should never be used as a "threat," that sound has probably stopped more thoughts of aggression than any other. The click of the safety being pushed "off" hardly makes any sound at all.

Veteran instructors may be found still teaching the old "port arms" and "shoulder-carry" positions. That's fine for close order drill in the Army but not really applicable to police work. Some may teach keeping your strong hand grasped at the pistol grip of the gun and swinging it up, so that the top of the receiver rests on your shoulder. The problem is two-fold. You can't see where the muzzle is pointing. And just watch a group of guys walking with guns on their shoulders. Before they've gone 50 yards, half of the guns will be dangling down at the end of their arms. If a carry isn't comfortable, guys won't use it. If they won't use it, why teach it?

8.2 Car-Carry Condition Trap

Suppose you grab the gun out of the vehicle gunlock. It's probably carried with the magazine tube loaded and action closed on an empty chamber with the safety on. You can bet the gun is cocked. *Under stress,* try to load it.

Carry 1: **Bill Burroughs demonstrates the carry common among sportsmen, when the situation is at ease. Crooked over your strong arm, the gun is in your field of view. You can see where the muzzle is pointing, at all times.**

Carry 2: Connecticut State Trooper Keith Price shows another carry, cradling the gun over your weak arm. Notice the advantage of the hand covering the trigger guard, and the disadvantage of the muzzle being out of your field of view. Your handgun hand is free for a fast draw if necessary.

Remember, the action is locked when the gun is cocked. You've got to push the action release (or pull the trigger if you're sure the gun is empty) before you can rack a shell into the chamber.

8.3 Situation Tenses

When the situation tenses, and you're in a position of imminent threat, the "ready" puts you in position for a quick reaction.

Obviously, for fastest response, the shotgun needs to be carried fully loaded and ready to fire. When the potential threat is right around the corner, the action is closed with a shell in the chamber and the safety "off"—with the trigger finger outside the trigger guard.

Ready Position: **When the situation is tense, the gun in the ready position is a split second away from being fired.**

8.4 Ready Position

The military foisted the "port arms" position on us. But it takes time to get the gun up to your shoulder when its butt is down by your hip. So we taught the recruit to straighten his weak arm to level the shotgun and fire it from the hip. Fairly accurate, but is it certain? Hardly.

John Satterwhite, a shotgun champion now with Heckler & Koch, learned a lesson from his experience in International Skeet.

"In this competition, the clay target is traveling at 100 mph. American skeet targets go 60 mph. The shooter must drop his stock to the level of his waist. And there can be up to three seconds delay after he calls for the bird," Satterwhite explains. "You don't really know when the target will present itself, and since they're all doubles, you have to get on that first bird in under half a second or you'll never have time to take the other one."

To be ready, the International Skeet shooter develops a technique that enables him to combine the three separate actions of mount, point, shoot, into *one* quick, smooth motion. It starts from what Satterwhite calls the "ready" position.

The application of such fast response shooting to police work is evident.

Try it. With your weak hand holding the fore-end and your strong hand at the pistol grip, bring the shotgun up to your cheek and pull it back into your shoulder, pointing at the target. Now, push it forward a bit and drop the stock to the level of your strong forearm. That's the "ready" position. You're looking through the front bead at the target. Gun loaded, safety off; but your trigger finger is outside the trigger guard.

From this position it takes almost no time to mount the gun and fire. In one test, shooters with only a little practice were firing in four-tenths of a second, including reaction time.

Even if the gun were to discharge unintentionally, the shot would go over the target's head. There might be a report to fill out but no personal injury damages to pay.

From the ready position, you're a split-second away from a well-aimed shot, should you need it.

9

Shooting the Shotgun

Shooting the shotgun should be a natural thing for you to do. If you can point your finger, you certainly can point a shotgun. It's when you pull the trigger that your shooting skills come into play. The principles are similar to many other recreational activities. So don't worry about learning them.

9.1 Pointing the Shotgun

The shooter looks at the target along the top of the shotgun barrel. Thus, you are not aiming the gun, but pointing it much as you would point your finger.

Keeping both eyes open provides you with the widest peripheral vision to detect new threats off to either side. Closing or squinting one eye narrows your field of vision and shuts off your ability to judge distance — depth perception. God gave you two eyes. Use them; unless you are right-handed with a left master eye, or vice versa.

With both eyes open, point your finger at something. Close your left eye. If your finger is not on-target, you've got a problem. One eye dominates the other. For most right-handers, the right eye is master. But I know guys who shoot a shotgun left-handed, even though they are right-handed, because their left eye is dominant.

Sighting in your shotgun is important. Bill Burroughs, left, explains that the rear shotgun sight is your eye. That's why it's important to anchor it to your cheek the same way each time you shoot. You must know where your individual gun shoots to employ it most effectively.

"I don't agree," says one instructor friend of mine. "You aim a shotgun the same as you do your handgun." He likes rifle-sighted slug barrels.

Rifle sights on a shotgun are handy when you're shooting slugs. But it's a rare case when you're shooting a rifled-slug at long range. So, if most of your shotgun work is going to be within 25 yards and with buck shot, I feel rifle sights get in the way. They're distracting. But if they're there, I use them like the handgun point-shoulder position—look through the sights at the target.

9.2 Trigger Slap

The desirable trigger action with a shotgun is better described as a "slap." When you shoot a double-action revolver, you don't think of the trigger action as separate parts. There's no "holding" while the gun wavers. It's a smooth stroke straight through to the end. Your shotgun trigger is single action, so it doesn't move much and it takes less pressure to set it off.

Watch out for the same problems you may have faced with the handgun, such as jerking the trigger. The consequences aren't as devastating with the shotgun, because you have more control over that long gun than you do the short one. Jerking the trigger, however, can still throw your shot off-target.

If you've developed a good trigger action with the revolver, you shouldn't have any trouble when you shoot the shotgun.

9.3 Lead and Swing

"It's a funny thing about shooting moving targets," an old time skeet instructor told me. "You don't shoot at the target. You shoot at where the target is going to be when the shot charge gets there."

When shooting at a moving target, you have to lead the target to compensate for the time it takes for the shot to travel from the gun to the target. It's like a paint brush. The brush handle actually points ahead of where the ends

Shooting clay targets is a good exercise to develop reaction. You quickly learn what it means to lead a moving target. Officer Jim Bergstrom of the Eden Prairie (Minn.) Police Department did it with his Choate pistol-grip Remington.

of the bristles touch the surface. When you water the lawn with a hose, you sweep the nozzle sideways, not in a straight line. Same principle when firing a shotgun. If lead (distance, not the stuff from which shot is made) were always a set number of yards, you could put a sight on the side of the gun. But it's not. How much you lead depends on the *speed* and *direction* of the target.

Only practice will develop the "feel" for the proper lead. The skeet shooter knows just how far to lead from each shooting station. His targets are always flying in the same path at a pre-set speed. But your target may be going away or crossing at an angle at who knows what speed. Rather than trying to mentally calculate proper lead for a particular situation, there's a technique that automatically compensates.

9.3.1 Swing-Through

Instead of holding a set lead on a moving target, you can eliminate all the technical calculations required for maintaining a fixed lead. Simply pace the speed of your gun muzzle just a bit faster than the apparent speed of the moving target. As the muzzle passes the target, your brain says, "shoot," and the action begins.

9.3.2 Follow-Through

Continuing a smooth swing, your reaction time automatically compensates for the variables of target speed and angle. The lead is determined by the speed of your reaction time. Remember, you are pacing the gun a bit faster than the apparent speed of the target. Slap the trigger as the gun passes through the target, and continue a smooth swing.

Follow-through is important. A smooth continuous motion is as vital to good shooting as it is to good golf, tennis, or baseball. It becomes the governing factor in applying swing-through on a moving target. Follow-through is what provides the lead needed to put the shot on target.

You'll develop a "feel" for just how fast to swing the gun to hit your target.

You can get some real practice mounting the shotgun and developing that "feel" for lead by using the conventional clay target games, but for a different purpose. The FBI Academy uses the skeet field to develop a trainee's reaction. In my instructor class, we had only a trap field available, so we shot from very unconventional positions. Then we quickly understood the concept of leading a moving target.

9.4 Hip-Shooting

It used to be taught that from the old "port arms" position, it's faster to deliver a close-range shot from the hip. Using the same grip on the gun, just straighten your left arm. The right elbow locks the stock of the gun into your side and the right forearm is parallel to the ground. Thus, the gun is level and can be pointed with fair accuracy at very close ranges. This isn't something you'd normally do with a shotgun, but it could be used for a reactive shot if you are jumped.

Because the odds are you'd never shoot from the hip, and since there's a better way to get off a quick close-quarter shot, there's no point in learning the hip-shooting technique. If the situation is at ease, you're using a sportsman's carry. If it's tense, you should be in the ready-position; then it's quicker to mount the gun to your shoulder to fire.

9.5 Skip-Firing

The fact that a projectile does not ricochet like a billiard ball, but travels a few inches away from a hard surface, taught us never to inch along an alley wall. This same characteristic can be used against a subject hiding behind an automobile—or inching along an alley wall.

Skip-firing refers to ricocheting a shot charge off the street one to three yards in front of the intended target. It can be used against the felon shooting at you from behind an automobile with his feet and ankles exposed, if he's standing between the tires.

Another theory is that the possibility of inflicting fatal wounds is reduced. Not necessarily so. When they ricochet, the pellets are deformed. They can fly off in any direction. When they hit, deformed pellets can cause more spectacular but usually less penetrating wounds. The buckshot you're loaded with on the street can still be deadly even after ricocheting off the pavement.

The shotgun is never used to "punish" an offender. It is used *only* when deadly force is justified.

9.6 Getting to Know Your Gun

How will you know where to point your shotgun if you don't know where it shoots? No two guns are identical twins, even those of the same make and model. Each has its own idiosyncrasies. Set up a blank piece of paper. Paint a dot on it for an aiming point. Then shoot one of the shells you normally carry in the gun. The center of the pattern is where your gun looks when it shoots. If that mid-point isn't on the aiming point, you'll need to make allowances.

Gunmakers check straightness of the shotgun barrel in the manufacturing process. If it's off the mark, the barrel is "influenced" with a barrel jack to make it right. Sighting through the bore at a light with a line through it, the workman sees a line running down the inside of the barrel. He turns the barrel to make sure the line is straight. If there's a bend in the line, he alters the barrel accordingly.

How far will your gun shoot? You have to try it. These bobber targets were set to just barely fall with a hit from a 9mm pistol bullet. Different guns, even of the same brands, failed to drop targets at different distances. The first gun to drop out was at 25 yards. One gun lasted back to 45 yards.

How far will your gun shoot effectively? You can't tell without shooting it.

We used a "popper" target for this test. That's a metal target hinged onto a base plate. It can be adjusted, based on the amount of force needed to knock it down. The one we shot at was adjusted so that it fell when hit by a 9mm bullet.

Then, with 00 Buck loads, each man in my instructor class started shooting at the target from increasing distances. Every one in the class dropped the target at 20 and 25 yards. A couple of men failed at 30 yards, more dropped out at 35 and 40 yards; one man made it all the way back to 45 yards before his target refused to fall. And guns used were 12-gauge pump models.

Shooting at a cardboard target or even firing a round of skeet during qualification time once- or twice-a-year is hardly enough to make you sufficiently familiar with the shotgun in your cruiser. It takes lots of practice to handle it professionally. Time well spent.

10

Shotgun in Combat

When you learn to shoot formal shotgun sports like trap and skeet, your coach explains the ritualistic shooting style, stance, gun position, and swing. Making a habit of these tailored techniques works well when the actions of the target are predetermined by the rules of the game.

In combat, there are no such rules. The scumbag shooting at you never heard of the Geneva Convention. The only rules he follows are those that affect his own survival, and that means taking you out by whatever means he can.

What you learn in shotgun training are principles, not absolutes. Principles always apply but should never get in the way of delivering a shot of salvation when you need it.

10.1 Mounting the Shotgun

In the ready position, the shotgun is held in both hands, pointing ahead (as in bayonet drill, for you old vets). Keep the front bead in your line of sight. When it comes time to fire, lift your strong elbow, bringing the stock up to your cheek; pivoting on the front bead, pull it back into the hollow of your shoulder, point and fire.

Through practice you will develop the ability to bring the shotgun into

Jerry Lane shows the sequence of a proper gun mount; it should be one quick, smooth motion for you. From the ready position. . .

the right elbow is raised, lifting the gun automatically up to your cheek and back into your shoulder. . .

until you are in a proper firing position.

We turned on the lights to show you what these guys did in the dark — once they had practiced a proper gun mount.

firing position on target. The secret is to focus your attention on the target, pivot on that front bead, and bring the gun up to your face. If you twist your head down to the stock, your eyes are at an angle and you can't see the target properly.

With the gun in proper position, you don't see the top of the barrel with the shooting eye. If you do, the gun is too low on your shoulder.

Just how fast can a shot be fired? My stopwatch hardly registered because of my own reaction time. Once members of the instructor class had practiced using their subconscious mind to shoot the gun, the shot was off as quickly as the gun hit the shoulder. From the "fire" command, the sound of the shot came in just four-tenths of a second, as near as I could tell.

But speed isn't the only advantage.

Once this technique had been practiced, instructors Bill Burroughs and Jerry Lane brought us into the indoor range, then they turned out the lights. There was barely enough of a glow to tell where the target was. There was no way you could see the sight. Yet, from the ready position, everyone in the class put every shot in the center mass of the target. Don't you wish you could do that?

You can. You need only to learn how to properly mount the shotgun and practice the procedure enough times to make it habit.

We spent half a day learning the carry position, the ready position, the loading position and mounting the gun — all before a single shot was fired. These exercises made the group "look good" with the gun. It stands to reason, if you exude an aura of skill and confidence, a bad guy may think twice before he tries to take you out.

A series of one-shot drills in getting a good gun mount followed. From the ready position (the front bead on the target and stock level with your forearm) bring the stock up to your cheek and back into the hollow of your shoulder by raising the strong elbow.

Everyone looked for a good sight picture before firing.

A five-minute lecture explained the workings of the subconscious mind. Then another one-shot drill followed. "This time I want to hear the gun fire as soon as the butt hits your shoulder," Burroughs said. After a few shots you could hear the difference, and the shots were still going onto the target.

10.2 Subconscious Mind

"Reaction time" is the time it takes for your brain to recognize a situation, make a decision, then instruct your muscles to move in reaction. Your conscious mind will take anywhere from three- to five-tenths of a second to complete this process.

Notice in your practice of mounting the gun and shooting, there's a split second of hesitation, while your brain checks the sight picture before your finger slaps the trigger.

Your subconscious mind works one-third faster than the conscious mind. If you practice a motor skill enough, you soon begin doing it without conscious thought. How many times have you driven a stretch of boring highway and suddenly realized you don't remember passing a point you know you passed. When you drive that car, you don't think about how much pressure to put on the brake pedal to stop the car. Your subconscious mind applies just the right amount of pressure you need.

It works the same in shooting the shotgun.

If you're a bird hunter and a bird flushes in front of you, do you calculate his direction, speed, and the amount of lead necessary to put your shot pattern where he is going to be when it gets there? Of course not. You swing the gun just a bit faster than the bird, slap the trigger as the muzzle passes the target, continuing a smooth swing.

If your attention is focused on a man drawing a gun on you, do you want to take the time to bring the gun up and consciously get a good sight picture? If you don't get a good sight picture you may miss the target — and you're dead. Letting the subconscious mind handle this task speeds up the process. The gun literally fires itself as the butt comes to your shoulder in a proper gun mount.

Once you've developed proper shooting skills, this application of the subconscious mind is developed by pushing yourself to shoot faster, but always with the gun under control.

If you push so hard you start losing control of the gun, Jerry Lane offers a remedy. "Slow down just one-tenth of a second," he said. "You'll wind up shooting faster."

10.3 Double Tap

With the handgun, you learn to double-tap — fire two quick shots — at a single adversary. You can do the same with the shotgun. You may have to. The whole purpose of shooting is to stop the aggressor's felonious act that endangers you or a third party. If the first shot doesn't stop him, the second one should.

The technique is simply two quick shots. You should develop the habit of quickly racking the action each time you shoot. Slap the trigger again as soon as the action is closed, and you've double-tapped the target.

10.4 Close Quarters

You're on a house search and an aggressor jumps out two feet away. You don't have room to mount the gun. Step back as you lock the stock under your

If you're approaching a door, you just aren't going to hold that shotgun at the ready. Pull it back toward your body, so you don't expose it to someone inside. If he should pop out. . .

jam the butt up under your armpit and shoot fast.

"Mounted ready" is another technique you might use in a building search. The gun is at your shoulder, but the muzzle is dropped out of harm's way.

armpit and pull the trigger. It's faster and much more accurate than the old hip-shooting technique.

If you are going through a door, bring the gun close to your body in a "port arms" position. Instinctively, you're just not going to push that muzzle past the door jamb where someone inside could grab it. Fine. When the scumbag jumps out, step back as you clamp the butt under your armpit, and pull the trigger.

You could peek around the corner with the gun already mounted on your shoulder, but with the muzzle pointed down, out of harm's way. It's called the "ready mount." It takes almost no time to raise the muzzle in line with the target, if you need to make a fast response.

10.5 Instinctive Shooting

There's no such thing as instinctive shooting. But you can learn to shoot instinctively — if you practice enough. It's hardly practical to pull a pistol and, from the hip, put a dinner plate-size six-shot group into a silhouette, while you're learning a faster technique that enables you to shoot a group that could be covered by a coffee cup.

When a threat becomes apparent, it takes little time to raise the muzzle . . .

into a quick firing position. Even though the cheek/butt anchor point is ignored, at close range you'll neutralize the threat.

That happened to me. I had practiced the hip-crouch so much that my shot group was smaller than my first efforts at close range in the Weaver stance. That's the way it was until I had practiced the stance enough to make its technique a habit, the natural thing to do. Then the Weaver groups were smaller.

If you have practiced an old shotgun technique so much that it feels natural, it may take a while to train yourself out of a bad habit.

Several years ago, when we were kids, we took our .22 rifles down to the town dump to help hold the rat population in check. It was great practice. I used an old Springfield .22 auto with a 2½ X scope. After a while I got pretty good at it. To this day, I credit that time spent down at the dumps with the ability to throw a scope-sighted deer rifle to my shoulder and see the deer through the scope.

One day we found a box of old medicine vials, small glass tubes a couple of inches long and perhaps a half-inch thick. Now there's a challenging target for a couple of kids with .22s. But no one wanted to wade out into the trash to set them up. We took turns throwing them out over the trash for each other to shoot at. After a while, we were holding the rifle at hip level, throwing the vials sidearm, then mounting the gun and blasting them to bits.

If memory serves me right, it took no more than a couple of hours and several boxes of ammunition to achieve that remarkable level of shooting skill. And that's as much credence as I'll give to the idea of instinctive shooting. The real name of the game is practice, practice, and more practice.

10.6 Walking and Searching

The techniques you use while hunting for a fugitive are determined by the tenseness of the situation. We've already talked about how to carry the shotgun, how to be ready when the situation tenses, and how to get off a quick shot.

But there's another little tip that hasn't been covered.

As the situation tenses, and you don't know where the threat might appear, you don't want to cross yourself up. Suppose you're moving to the left. You step with your right foot over to the left, crossing your left leg. Suddenly, an aggressor jumps out to your right. You've got to shuffle your feet to turn in that direction, and that takes just enough time to get you killed.

If the situation is that tense, don't cross your legs. Sidewise movement is better by bringing one foot up to the other. Do the shuffle and keep yourself always in balance.

10.7 Pivot

You're watching a suspect, standing in an "interview" position with the shotgun at the ready. Suddenly, from one side—either side—an accomplice

Sgt. Curt Oberlander of the Eden Prairie (Minn.) Police Department had been walking toward the left when, suddenly, a target turned hostile. Simply look and pivot the whole body as you mount the gun. It's fast. Burroughs called the hostile target.

steps out from behind a dumpster and raises his gun. Simply look at the target, pivot your whole body while mounting the gun, and fire.

That look is important. Not only must you look to identify the threat, but you must look at the target in mounting the gun. The procedure is look, mount, fire. Use the same procedure when the target is off to the side, and your shot is virtually as fast as shooting to the front. The pivoting and mounting are combined into one smooth motion, and the subconscious mind takes care of shooting the gun.

If the threat comes from behind you, you've got to turn. The quickest turn is to swing your left foot (for right-handers) 180 degrees, pivoting on your strong foot, as you mount and fire. Notice that this turn keeps the gun tucked in close, and gives it a punching motion directly toward the target. If you turned to the right, you'd have to swoop the muzzle around and try to stop its sidewise swing on the target. Mirror-image for left-handers.

10.8 Using Cover

Running through the tactical cover course that your instructor sets up with props on the range gets you in the *habit* of looking for cover. If all your

Barricade shooting means taking advantage of cover. Officer Mario Chapa of the Hammond (Ind.) Police Department keeps his body behind the mailbox while he takes out the hostile target. He's far enough back from the cover that, leaning to his left, he took out the other target, too.

A tactical cover course can get you in the habit of looking for cover — when you know where the danger lies. There were seven different shooting stations on this set-up, and we had to run from one to the other.

training is on an open range, you may react the same under stress and ignore a safer place nearby to shoot from. Practice firing from behind a mailbox, tree (from each side), wall, curbing, garbage can or fire hydrant while you run from one shooting position to another.

10.8.1 Crossover

But what about firing around the left corner of the building, for you right-handers? Do you do the mirror-image routine you practiced on the pistol range? It isn't as easy with the long gun.

Rather than trying to shoot offsided, under stress you'll keep the gun on your right shoulder, sight with your right master eye, and simply lean backwards to pop around the corner and shoot. So why not practice it that way? It makes sense to keep doing what you've always been doing.

Crossover shooting is a lot easier than it looks. When a dozen instructors in our class tried it, they found no problem maintaining balance, nor were they knocked over backwards. From the first shot, they easily delivered a shot right on target from around the offside of the cover. So what if the stance looks funny. It works.

10.8.2 Where's the Beef?

Talk all you want about using cover, you still may not transfer that idea to a realistic situation that's different. Suppose you don't know where the threat lies. What's cover then?

After we had gone twice through the tactical cover course, we were taken, one by one, to the edge of the woods.

"For safety's sake, a student instructor will be right behind you," Bob Hunt explained. "That's so you don't turn and shoot back at a target you may have passed. White markers indicate the general direction you should move. From there, you're on your own."

All of a sudden, we didn't know where the targets were. With a long gun in their hands, more than a few reverted to deer-hunting techniques. I slowly sneaked straight through a clearing inviting fatal consequences. The first steel target I saw was too far away to drop with the birdshot we were using. It didn't fall. I had to get closer, watching for other adversaries along the way. Finally, I remembered to use the tactics learned earlier.

But the confusion of facing a situation different from the regimen on the range taught me an important lesson that will never be forgotten.

10.9 Advantage of Knowing Your Gun

If you know your individual gun, and are really familiar with it, you'd be amazed at what you can do with it. You need to know exactly where your gun

From behind cover, with a target to either side, it's fastest to "cross over." Simply lean back enough for an effective shot; never mind the stance.

These guys had never fired a "crossover" before, but no one had any trouble taking out targets on either side of the "tree."

To build confidence, each man in the class erased the face of the hostile hostage taker, to the rear, holding a gun to our partner's head in front.

shoots, how big the pattern is at different distances, and you need to shoot it enough to instill confidence.

Strictly as a confidence-building exercise, we set up an intolerable situation. Two metal "poppers," targets that fall when hit, were placed one partially behind the other. The face of the rear target was exposed, a face about the same size as mine. Suppose that the rear target is a scumbag holding a gun at your partner's temple as he says, "I'm gonna blow your partner away, and I want you to watch."

You're standing 10 yards away with your shotgun in the ready-position, loaded with 00 Buck. It's a situation where your partner is as good as dead.

After running through all of these combat exercises, everyone in class could put a saucer-size pattern of nine .33 caliber pellets right in the face of the foe without touching the good guy in front, firing the instant the gun butt hit the shoulder.

You can imagine the effect of an instantaneous frontal lobotomy. The guy wouldn't even have time for a death reaction of pulling the trigger.

11

Handling Malfunctions

With the reliability of modern pump guns, you may never experience a jam. But anything's possible. Just work the shotgun with purpose and you'll avoid problems. Don't "baby" a shotgun action. That could lead to "short stroking" the action. This means the bolt doesn't return fully to the rear, so it misses the shell on the lifter and closes on an empty chamber.

You wear your sidearm at all times. You load and unload it every day. You can "dry-fire" it in front of the bedroom mirror if you're conscientious. You fire a full qualification course regularly. You're familiar with your handgun. But the shotgun stays locked in the rack in the cruiser. Even if you have to remove it and unload it after your patrol, you probably get little chance to shoot it on the range. You never walk around with the shotgun the way you do your handgun. You have little opportunity to get really acquainted with your shotgun, so that you know what to do with it when something goes wrong.

11.1 Identify the Problem

If you're suddenly faced with a malfunction in a stressful situation, uncertainty and fumbling efforts to clear the problem could cause an undesirable statistic. You must take a second to determine what the problem is. Once you know it, you act accordingly, or know if you should fall back to the secondary weapon on your hip.

If the fired shell in the chamber fails to extract, you wind up with this. If you can shake the back shell out and rack the action again, fine. But if you're threatened, drop it and use your handgun.

It's best to become familiar with what can happen and practice quick fixes. You can't afford indecision in combat.

11.2 Failure to Extract

If the extractor breaks or gets so cruddy it doesn't engage the rim of the shell, the bolt may open without pulling the fired shell out of the chamber. Rack the action again, if you have time. If not, go to the handgun because what you're holding is a three-foot club.

Later you can pick the shell out of the chamber with a knife, or drop a cleaning rod down the bore to knock out the fired shell. Then clean or replace the extractor.

11.3 Failure to Eject

It's possible that the ejector could break. It's even possible that you could work the action so fast that the spent shell is caught by the closing bolt. Then you have a "stovepipe" sticking out of the ejection port. For whatever reason it happens, you must get rid of it in the shortest possible time.

In your excitement, you rack the action so fast the bolt starts to close before the ejected shell clears the port.

Pull the action open again, and wipe the "stovepipe" shell away.

The quick fix is simple. Pull the action back all the way and wipe the spent shell away with a quick rearward swipe of your weak hand, then close the action.

11.4 Double Feed

The shell stop could break or be so dirty it fails to hold shells in the magazine tube. More likely, you just didn't push it in far enough. If two shells come out of the tube, you have one shell on the carrier and the rear of another shell pushing against it from the front. You can't close the action.

So just stick your finger in through the ejection port and push the offending shell forward until you hear it "click" past the shell stop.

11.5 Stacked Feed

The action is closed and a shell slips past the shell stop and gets between the closed bolt and the carrier. It used to be inherent with pump gun design, a real problem. But no more.

With earlier Remington 870s, the only way to clear this stoppage was to punch out the two drift pins holding the trigger group and remove it to drop out the offending shell. Remington made a design change in guns manufactured at the end of 1984, so this is no longer a potential malfunction.

A Remington 870 sold after January 1985 is of the new design and can be identified by looking at the shell carrier. Those with the new "Flexitab" modification have a U-shaped cut in the carrier.

Older guns can be converted by the department armorer with one of two inexpensive kits offered by Remington. One includes a complete breech bolt assembly. The other has the bolt by itself, so you can use the internal parts from the old bolt.

The Ithaca even has a split carrier so you can use a knife through the slot to push the offending shell back into the magazine tube—if you have time.

My introduction to this innovation was at the SHOT Show in Atlanta in 1982. S&W's former eastern regional manager for law enforcement, Tom Madden, demonstrated the then-new Model 3000 Police shotgun. He loaded a dummy shell into the chamber and closed the action. Then he stuffed another dummy into the magazine tube and tripped the shell stop, so that the second shell slipped back into the action between the lifter and the bolt.

"You've had it now," I said.

He just smiled as he "fired" the dummy in the chamber, racked the action and "fired" the second dummy that supposedly had jammed the action. The key is to rack the action with purpose.

If you're in a combat mode and this condition jams your old gun, you have only one course of action.

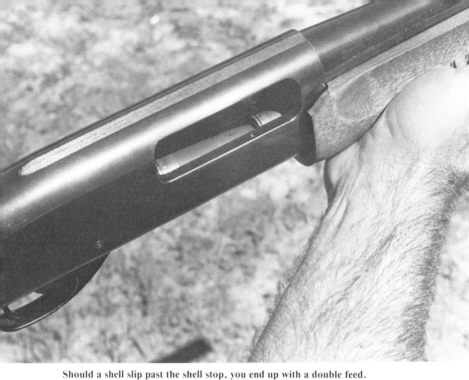

Should a shell slip past the shell stop, you end up with a double feed.

Simply reach in and push the offending shell forward, until the shell stop catches it.

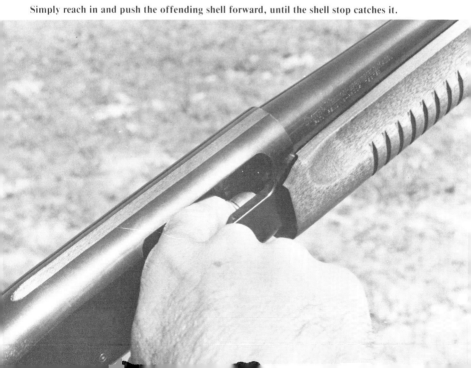

If your gun is an older one and won't function in a "stacked feed" situation, you have only one choice. With your finger holding the action release and other hand firmly on the fore-end. . .

slam the butt down on a hard surface. If that doesn't clear it, use your handgun.

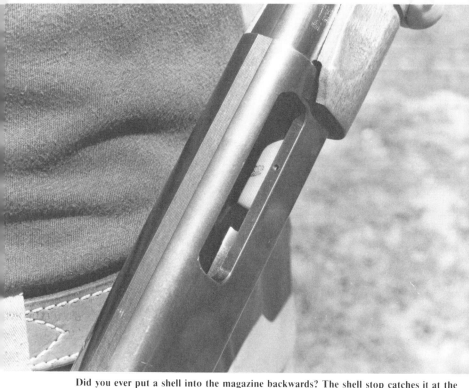

Did you ever put a shell into the magazine backwards? The shell stop catches it at the wrong end. . .

a finger through the ejection port pushes the shell back into the tube, while another finger pushes the lifter up. . .

until the offending shell drops out.

Get a firm grip on the fore-end, wrap your strong hand around the trigger guard, and depress the slide release. Then kneel and slam the butt of the gun against a hard surface. So what if the stock breaks. You can shoot the gun with two hands, if need be. At least you'll be able to shoot it.

11.6 Backward Shell

You can tell by touch which way the shell is pointing. But suppose the inexplicable happens and a shell goes into the magazine tube backwards? Instructor Jerry Lane discovered quite by accident one day that there *is* a way out of this dilemma, if you have time.

On shotguns with two shell stops, one functions when the action is open, the other when it's closed. There is a point between the two where neither is extended. Move the slide slowly until you find that point, reach in through the ejection port with one finger, and push the offending shell back into the tube. While you hold it, push the shell carrier up past the shell with the other hand and drop the backward shell out. If the backward shell gets onto the carrier, stick a finger in through the ejection port and push it down all the way. Then you can roll the gun onto its side and drop the shell out.

All this reminds me of a story told me by the late H. E. "Tiny" Helwig of

Winchester-Western when it was a division of Olin. As a shooting promoter, he lectured youth groups about gun safety. Once a mother came up to him after his talk and said, "If this sport is so dangerous you have to give a talk on safety, I don't want my child involved."

"Safety isn't really a separate subject," Tiny explained. "If one is learning to shoot, safety is simply part of doing it properly. But with a group of kids who don't know guns, we need to make them *aware*."

That's why shotgun stoppages rate their own chapter. You need to be *aware*. You need to be able to quickly identify a malfunction and apply the quick fix, or know that you must fall back on your secondary weapon without wasting time.

12

How to Get Good with Your Shotgun

Learning any motor skill is a matter of *proper* practice; that's just as true for the shotgun. But "proper" practice means it may not be something you can just go out and do yourself. If you practice a bad habit, it becomes difficult to unlearn. So practice under the watchful eye of your instructor, or someone whom you respect for his shotgun skills. If your instructor volunteers range time with department ammunition, provided you do it on your own time, it's worth it to you to take advantage of his offer.

If that doesn't work out, there's a group of people who shoot more shotshells than anyone else. They're usually very receptive to interested neophytes, and there's always one man there who gets his fun out of coaching a new shooter. They hang out at a place called a Rod & Gun Club or Sportsman's Club and they shoot the shotgun games called trap and skeet.

Now, they won't understand the way you use a shotgun. But they do understand shotguns and moving targets. And you can spend more shotshells in one afternoon at the gun club than either your shoulder or pocketbook can stand.

Trap and skeet are fun games. They're structured competition. Because they present you with movement and a variety of flying clay targets, one round of 25 shots will pass quickly. But just look at how much experience you gain in handling the gun, mounting it properly, and swinging on a moving target. If you can afford to take the family to the movies, you can afford to shoot a round or two of trap or skeet at your local gun club.

12.1 Trap

In the first quarter of the last century, a group of country squires in England got the idea of putting live pigeons under a row of old beaver hats. At the command "Pull!" an attendant pulled a string toppling the hat and releasing the bird. The shooter, standing a safe distance behind the row of hats, tried to hit the flying bird with his muzzleloading shotgun.

The top hats gave way to small iron traps that sprung open on the pull of a string. Thus, the name "trap."

Live pigeon shooting didn't sit well with some interests. Sportsmen themselves demand that the game has a fair chance. So, while live bird shoots are still held in some parts of the world, the game evolved to inanimate targets.

In the 1860s a machine was devised to throw glass balls filled with feathers. But the shooters of the day considered them a poor substitute.

By the 1880s, George Ligowski was watching some small boys skimming clam shells over the water and he was inspired. He devised a saucer-shaped clay target and a crude, spring-operated thrower. From those beginnings, trapshooting evolved.

This superimposed skeet and trap field at the Hartford (Conn.) Gun Club serves both purposes. Ignore the low traphouse in the middle. These gunners are shooting skeet (station 8) at the moment.

Trap uses one target-throwing machine, a "trap," in one low dugout traphouse, 16 yards in front of a fan-shaped pattern of five shooting stations.

One trap game is shot from the 16-yard line at a single target. But the trap oscillates or is indexed to a different position each time it is triggered. You never know which direction the target will take, except they always go *away* from you. This is where the beginner starts.

There are five shooting positions on the arc. You shoot five shells from one position then move to the next. Five times five is twenty-five and that's how many shells are in a box.

Doubles is fired from the 16-yard line, but two targets are thrown at the same time and fly at different angles. Skilled doubles-shooters usually take the bird closest to straightaway first, then go after the angled "bird." They generally agree this is the toughest clay target game.

Handicap is for the more skilled competitors. Based on their past performance in registered shoots, shooters are handicapped by having to shoot at distances greater than 16 yards. That's why the trap field looks like a fan with ribs all the way back to 27 yards.

The trapshooter is permitted to mount his gun before he calls for the bird. If you really want your best score in the beginning, go ahead. But remember your interest is a bit different. Once you get good at breaking targets at the 16-yard line, try starting from the police ready-position. It's more meaningful practice for you.

Frankly, trap is a serious sport. In competition, shooters on the line can become perturbed if a bumbler breaks the rhythm of the squad. And trap shooting calls for a full-choke gun to reach out and break those difficult angles. So, skeet shooting is more suitable for police training.

12.2 Skeet

Skeet is a more relaxed sport. It came into being about 1915 when a group of sportsmen tried to devise a clay target game that more closely approximates actual upland game hunting. It was first called "clock-shooting" because the shooter moves "around the clock."

There are two traphouses in skeet, a high house to the left and a low house to the right. Shooting stations are in a semi-circle that ranges from one house to the other. Station 1 is directly in front of the high house. Stations 2 and 3 are further around the circle, station 4 in the 90 degree spot, stations 5 and 6 and then 7 directly in front of the low house. Then to add insult to injury, station 8 is in the center, between the two trap houses. Targets fly almost directly overhead and you have to break them before they pass you.

While the targets always fly in the same path, the shooter moves. He is presented with targets at every angle; outgoing, incoming, and crossing. The squad of up to five shooters takes turns at each shooting station, so there's more time for casual conversation.

Starting at station 1, you take one target from each house, one and then the other. This is repeated all the way around the circle. Then you come back to station 1 for your first doubles. Targets are thrown from each house at the same time. Break the going away bird first then turn on the incomer. Doubles are repeated at stations 2, 6, and 7.

All this adds up to 24 shots. Your twenty-fifth shell in the box is an optional shot. The first target you miss, you can shoot it again. Someday you'll make it all the way around without a miss. Then you can take your optional shot from any point you wish.

Because skeet calls for a more open-choked gun, it's better suited to your practice with the police shotgun than is trap. And you'd be surprised how well you can do with that short barrelled gun. At the IALEFI conference in Nashville in 1984, Norm Wilson of Remington ran the visiting instructors through a session at skeet using only police model shotguns. He pointed out the advantages for the police trainee and the attending instructors agreed.

In skeet, you must start with the shotgun off the shoulder. In International Skeet, the butt must be down by your waist. When you see the target, you have to mount the gun and break the moving bird quickly before it gets away. See the similarity with the police situation?

12.3 Personal Practice

The only way you'll become familiar with your shotgun is by shooting it. So make a game of it.

There are inexpensive practice traps. Trius Products of Cleveland, Ohio, makes a line of excellent clay target and tin-can throwers. Your instructor will want to requisition one to save his arm. Handtraps are least expensive, but you supply the throwing power.

If your partner wants some shotgun practice, too, you've got it made. Take turns throwing clay targets for each other in any old field where it's safe to shoot. Set your own rules. Best out of ten targets, or five when your arm gets tired. Throw doubles. Lob three clay birds up high and break each before it hits the ground. Remember, Herb Parsons could toss seven and break each in succession with a pump gun.

The shooting session should be fun. Enjoy it. The fact that you gain experience with the gun, handling it safely with others around, and sharpen your shooting skills shouldn't detract at all from your personal practice.

13

Keeping Your Shotgun

The detective has good information that the wanted man is in that warehouse. He warns, "He's armed and dangerous." A sergeant rolls up with another backup unit. Exits are covered. The building is supposedly clear of innocent bystanders. But the man you're after isn't one to flush easily.

"Break out the shotguns," the sergeant says.

Now you're faced with doing a building search in a honeycomb of aisles and passages that interlace the pallets of crates and boxes on the warehouse floor. You've learned to use the ready-position with the shotgun when a threat is imminent.

"That's one of the four situations where an attempt to disarm the officer with a shotgun is likely to occur," says Robert K. Lindsey, a retired captain from the Jefferson Parish, Louisiana Sheriff's Department. He's now Director of Organizational and Individual Development with Wells Fargo Guard Services. "The other situations occur when the shotgun malfunctions, when you're reloading and when you're in a 'don't-shoot' situation."

Lindsey has made a study of shotgun retention, and everything he can learn about officer survival. With good reason.

If you remember the infamous sniper incident on the roof of the Howard Johnson Hotel in New Orleans a few years ago, you recall that three officers were killed. Those were Lindsey's men. He vowed that it would never happen again.

Since then, he has sought knowledge with a passion. He has learned from the best teachers in defensive tactics, but he didn't take what he heard for granted. He tried techniques, tested different ideas, and improved on what he learned. While Jim Lindell of the Kansas City, Missouri Police had developed a handgun-retention system, no one had addressed the concern of the shotgun. So Bob Lindsey did.

"The problem is that the usual self-defense techniques, by themselves, are not the answer to retaining the long gun," Lindsey says.

Using his knowledge of defensive tactics and the martial arts, he developed four simple procedures that virtually insure your retaining the shotgun when an assailant tries to grab it (a) from the front or off-side, (b) from the strong side, (c) from the front with the gun at port arms, or (d) from the rear.

We'll give you the gist of his shoulder weapon retention system but this, like all defensive tactics, should be learned and practiced under the watchful eye of a qualified instructor. Besides, even when sales are restricted, periodi-

Bob Lindsey, in the Wells Fargo T-shirt, developed the techniques to retain your shoulder gun. He demonstrates for his new boss, H. M. Leith. The Wells Fargo Protection Force and Special Response Teams guard the nation's Strategic Petroleum Reserve. *Julie Madden, WFGS.*

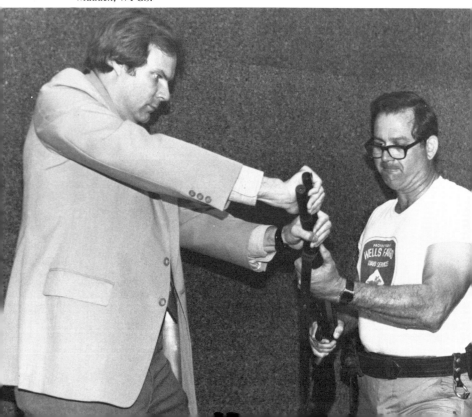

cals and publications have a way of reaching the wrong hands. So there is one aspect of Lindsey's techniques that has never appeared in print.

"The key to all defensive tactics is to react immediately to an attack," Lindsey explains. "The officer must have practiced a planned response, so that he uses it instinctively and decisively."

13.1 Grab from Front or Off-side

You're at a corner in the hallway. The subject steps out, grabs your shotgun, and tries to pull it away from you.

Use the force of his pull to your own advantage. React immediately by stepping forward with the off-foot, and thrust the barrel toward the attacker. Then quickly step forward with the strong foot, forcing the butt of the gun downward. Then step past the attacker with the off-foot while thrusting the barrel toward the outside of the attacker's body and reach. The final move is to create distance. *Get out of his reach* so he can't grab the gun again.

13.2 Grab from the Strong Side

As you approach the open door on your strong side, the scumbag reaches out and grabs your shotgun.

Immediately step forward with the off-foot, thrusting the barrel forward. Shove the butt downward and toward the outside as you step forward with the strong foot. Then pivot yourself and the shotgun toward the outside of the attacker's body. *Create distance.*

13.3 Grab from the Front, Gun in Port Arms

Immediately step forward with the off-foot, thrusting the barrel upwards. Then step forward with the strong foot, while quickly shoving the butt forward and toward the outside. Step forward again with the off-foot and push the barrel toward the outside of the attacker's body. *Create distance.*

13.4 Grab from the Rear

This is a reverse application of what's gone on before. Immediately step backward with the strong foot, thrusting the butt downward and toward the outside. Pivot toward the attacker, while shoving the barrel toward the outside of the attacker's body. Then step back and to the side with the strong foot, pulling the gun in close to yourself. *Create distance.*

Grab from front. *Sgt. Lloyd Babin, Jefferson Parish (Louisiana) Sheriff's Department.*

Grab from strong side.
Babin.

 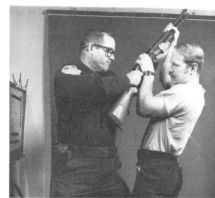

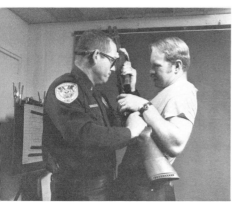 

Grab from front, port arms. *Babin.*

Grab from rear. *Babin.*

Gun malfunctions. Grab your handgun!

13.5 Grab When Gun Malfunctions

The scumbag sees you've got a stovepipe jam, and he takes advantage of your predicament. Quickly rack the action back, wipe the shell away, and close the action.

By that time your gun is in the port arms position and the aggressor has his hands on it. Now follow the sequence above for port arms release.

13.6 Added Advice

"The officer with a shotgun must be continually aware of his surroundings. Weapon-retention is enhanced by being alert and ready to react instantly and instinctively," Lindsey says. "Never allow an attacker to get a death grip on your gun."

14

A Fun Challenge

Long ago, handgun trainers developed a pistol course that shooters found to be fun: the Practical Pistol Course. It soon became a competition, as structured as the old National Match Course, and moved away from being "training-oriented."

So the International Practical Shooting Confederation (IPSC) was formed to present more realistic situations in a type of competition that emphasizes hits, speed, and power, and deemphasizes precision accuracy. It has also become a competition, so it, too, isn't the ultimate "training" course.

Part of this handgun course, however, has been applied to the shotgun. It was more challenging and as exciting than any deer hunt I've been on.

14.1 The Course

A "jungle lane" course can be a series of situations that require fast decisions. What makes it a challenge is that you don't know where the targets are, how many there are, how long the course is, nor exactly what situations you'll face.

It takes some expertise to lay out such a course so it can be shot safely. This isn't something you'd want to do for yourself. Besides, if you set it up, you'd know where the targets are — and that's no fun.

The Agawam (Mass.) Pistol Club spiced up one IPSC match. They added a "jungle lane" in the woods next to the range. But this "jungle lane" was to be fired with shotgun slugs. At the start of the path, you were issued a short-barreled shotgun and 15 slug loads. But that didn't mean there were 15 targets. You might have to shoot a target more than once to be sure of taking it out, so you knew you had "some" extra shells.

"A safety officer will be right behind you just to be sure you don't swing back on a target toward the range," Dwight Brouillard said. "I'll be behind him timing you."

A captain with the Hampden County (Mass.) Sheriff's Office, Brouillard is an avid IPSC shooter. But he recognized the inadequacy of shotgun training in too many departments. He had run "jungle lanes" before for handguns, and saw its great potential for shotgun.

14.2 The Challenge

"There are blaze marks on trees to guide you, but do what you have to do to use cover, take out hostile targets — there may be hostages — and keep your gun loaded," he instructed.

A "jungle lane" course may be nothing more than some targets set in a safe manner in the woods. It's another ballgame when you don't know where the threat will appear.

Scanning the area before stepping out, we detected nothing. We crept up the path, stopping behind trees to look ahead before moving on. After rounding one clump of bushes, I thought I saw something off to the right. I dropped to one knee and stared. Yes, a camouflaged square didn't fit the scenery and camouflage meant hostile. One shot would take care of the situation, I thought.

Moving on, we passed another tree and hidden right behind it was a hostile target, not three feet away. There was no time nor space to do anything but bring the stock up under my armpit and shoot. I fired and saw the hole in that target.

Partly hidden in another clump of bushes was a pair of targets, a camouflage hostile half behind a plain brown hostage, maybe 30 yards away. A tree about ten feet ahead would give me cover and a better angle to shoot from, so I sneaked up on that tree, keeping out of the target's sight. I was confident of that shot, too.

In all, I figured there were eight targets but knew my time would be slow. This was competition, not training. My score was considerably fewer than eight dead hostiles. Five, if I recall correctly, and the time was slow. I had spent ten shells. A couple of targets needed extra convincing. If they hadn't, my score would have been fewer than five dead targets. Some shots, that I thought were good, were just outside the "K" zone and they don't count.

The walk back to the starting point, scoring and pasting targets on the way, gave me time to puff. My nerves were still on edge when I handed the shotgun to the next poor soul being subjected to the challenge of a "jungle lane."

14.3 The Score

It was fun, more of a challenge than I had thought it would be. When Brouillard critiqued my performance, it turned out to be a training experience as well. He scored me fairly well on tactics, using available cover. But I had completely overlooked a couple of targets. There had been ten. He scored me well on using a fast-response technique for that close surprise target. But I had killed one hostile by shooting through a hostage I never saw.

My only consolation is that I did as well as most of the guys who don't do this sort of thing every day.

15

Blowing Smoke with the Shotgun

The shotgun-armed officer could be faced with using chemical agents in connection with his shotgun. An introduction to the subject, if nothing more, should be included in shotgun training.

Our shotgun instructor class had been going through pivot practice, a tactical cover course, or "jungle lane," and it was time for something different. The routine was broken with chemical agents.

The instructor opened a box of normal-looking 12-gauge shells. But they were color-coded grey. That tells you they're chemical agent practice shells.

All chemical agent devices are color-coded to tell you what's inside. Red means CN, blue is CS, yellow is HC or smoke, green is DM, and grey means practice items. Violet is CR, a new chemical agent not used in the United States. You probably will never use DM, which is a sickening agent used by the military. We list them so you'll know what all the colors mean.

On the range, we set up a slab of plywood and each instructor took his turn punching a hole in it with those practice Ferret shells. It was the same as shooting slugs.

Then the instructor clamped what looked like a tin can on the muzzle of the shotgun. "This is a grenade launcher," he said. Taking a practice grenade he showed how to put it into the launcher with the safety lever under a tab on the launcher to hold it down. Only then can you pull the pin. But don't do it just yet.

The shotgun can handle large mobs. Instructor Ralph Maresco directs Officer Ralph Angeletta in launching a grenade some 300 yards downrange. Both are with Westchester County (N.Y.) Police.

15.1 Launching Grenades

Launching a grenade with a shotgun isn't like shooting a slug. It's like firing a mortar.

First, you must use a special launching cartridge. Otherwise, you might create an embarrassing situation. Felt recoil is more than shooting a slug, and the heavy grenade isn't going to fly like a bullet. The proper technique is to kneel, put the butt of the stock on the ground by your knee, and straighten your left arm to direct the muzzle. Then your partner, standing behind you, pulls the pin on the grenade and tells you to move the muzzle up, down, right, or left, just like the mortar fire controller.

It quickly became a game to see who could hit the log 300 yards downrange, or get even greater distance. One team put its practice grenade onto the backstop, and another actually hit the log.

Blowing smoke with the shotgun isn't difficult, as you can see, but it does take some practice so you know what to expect.

15.2 Chemical Agent Shells

Say some scumbag is holed up in a hotel room. You've isolated the area and officers are positioned outside where they can see the window into the room. The SWAT team is in the inside hallway waiting to bash through the door. The lieutenant decides to put gas into the room.

Well, if SWAT's there, you probably have a 37mm shoulder gas gun available and will use that. It throws a larger projectile with a greater amount of chemical agent. But suppose you're the local patrol and all you've got is your shotgun. If you've got a 12-gauge CA kit in your trunk, you can still be the gas man.

Ferret liquid agent barricade-penetrating cartridges, made by AAI Corporation, enable an officer with a shotgun to deliver a 3cc mixture of CS or CN agent into a hideout room or automobile interior. The Ferret will penetrate an automobile windshield or ¾-inch plywood at 100 feet. From 300 feet, it will penetrate quarter-inch plate glass, a hollow-core door or double-panel storm window and screen.

No special training is needed to use this cartridge but you should, at least, have fired some practice shells so you know where your gun shoots that little finned "bomb." Practice shells, color-coded grey, are offered with a red dye filler so you can tell where you hit.

15.3 Chemical Agents

During World War I, the U.S. Army spent a lot of time developing an inoffensive chemical agent suitable for training the troops with gas masks. Come to think of it, when I went through boot camp in World War II, we had to go through the gas house. It was enough to make a grown man cry.

The substance developed was *chloraceteophenone,* just remember it as CN. That's tear gas, a lacrimating agent, color-coded red. When a person is exposed to it, his tear ducts flow, his eyes smart, and his eyelids try to close. A burning sensation is felt on moist skin. Get away from the gas and the effects

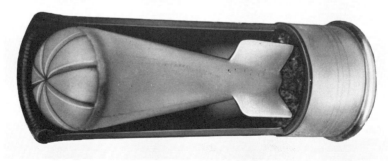

AAI's Ferret turns your shotgun into a gas gun. The cutaway shows the finned projectile inside. *AAI Corp.*

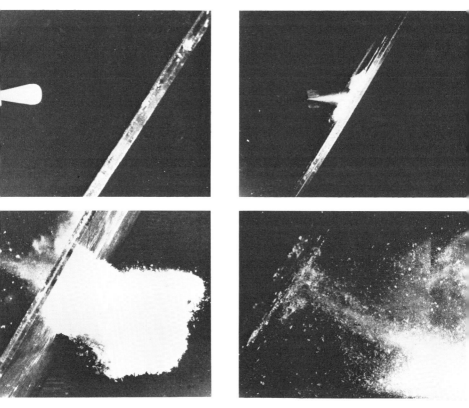

This four-photo sequence shows the ferret penetrating an automobile windshield. *AAI Corp.*

soon dissipate. Flushing with water helps. There are no adverse aftereffects, and it's relatively easy to clean up an area after exposure.

While we use the term "gas," tear gas is really a solid, a fine powder "dust" that is carried by something else; smoke in a grenade or liquid in an aerosol container.

In 1960, the U.S. Army adopted a new chemical agent called *orthochlorbenzalmalonontrile*. Remember it as CS, color-coded blue. This is an agent more potent than CN, an irritant that's more effective than CN against a large mob. The effects of CS include extreme burning sensation of the eyes, flowing tears, involuntary closing of the eyes, coughing and chest tightening, sinus and nasal drip, extreme burning sensation on areas of moist skin such as the face, armpits, and groin. If you use it indoors, it's more difficult to clean up than CN.

Another agent was available at that time but was considered too dangerous for law enforcement use: *diphenylaminechlorarsine*. Remember it as DM, color-coded green. It was developed in Germany in 1913. DM, also called *adamsite* in the United States, is a sickening agent with effects both dangerous and painful.

Another agent you may use is HC or smoke, color-coded yellow. This is simply the carrier smoke with no chemical agent, and can be used to obscure the subject's view of approaching officers. You know, the old smokescreen trick.

15.4 First Aid

It's probably your department policy that if you gas someone, you have to provide first aid. Fortunately, some commonsense practices apply to both CN and CS.

Remove the subject to a clear area and face him into the wind. Don't let him rub or scratch. This only pushes the particulates deeper into the skin. This is usually enough if exposure isn't severe. Flushing the eyes with cool, clear water will speed recovery, but tell him to use ten times as much water as he feels necessary. Always remove contact lenses before flushing the eyes.

If his clothing has become contaminated, take them off. You can pick up the agent on your hands and contaminate yourself. Normal cleaning will restore his clothing. Obviously, don't use any creams, salves, or dressings on irritated skin. That just traps the agent and prolongs its effects.

Exposure to chemical agents makes it seem as if you can't get your breath. That's a psychological effect on normal people. But if someone is showing signs of severe or prolonged effects, difficulty breathing, severe chest pain, or contamination of wounds, get medical help.

15.5 A Word of Caution

Chemical munitions are intended to be non-lethal. But if a Ferret shell will penetrate three-quarters of an inch of plywood, you can imagine what it would do to someone standing nearby. Even a muzzle blast discharge of nothing but gas from a 37mm gas gun could be devastating to someone's eyes at close range. A continuous discharge grenade burns with a fire hot enough to melt the fuse. You can imagine what it would do if lobbed into the trash in a tenement room.

If you have not been adequately trained with chemical agents by your department, leave the decision-making to someone who has.

16

Tender Loving Care

Inept care and cleaning of a gun can cause more problems than it solves. Bore wear from an improperly used cleaning rod can be more damaging than speeding bullets. But inattention to the condition of your gun can cause problems, too.

My old .38 Special target revolver has the wide hammer and trigger popular among bullseye shooters. It sports custom-fitted Lou Sanderson grips, and hasn't been used much in recent years. So a squirt of oil from a spray can down into the hammer hole should keep the rust away.

One day I took it out to check it. The action wouldn't function.

Not being a gunsmith, I violated my own rule and removed the sideplate to see what the problem was. My sprays of oil had kept the rust away all right but it had attracted dust, and the oil had solidified to a soft varnish. You could say I had "gummed up the works." A thorough cleaning and application of a *light* film of oil put the revolver back in working order.

How many guys have you seen squirt oil down into the action to avoid taking the gun apart?

"I'd rather not oil the gun at all than to use too much oil," said Don Vivenzio, instructor at Smith & Wesson's Armorers School. "For that reason, I don't like spray cans. You can too easily spray too much. Use a simple squeeze bottle, so you can put on just one drop of oil."

Vivenzio gave our shotgun instructor class an afternoon of tearing the guns down, showing where problems might arise and how to properly maintain the shotguns. It's not as complicated as you might think.

16.1 Troubleshooting

The shotgun performs four main functions: to feed, fire, extract, and eject a shell. While mechanical failure is rare, abuse of the police shotgun could lead to problems. And "abuse" includes inattention. Failure in any one of these functions points to a problem with the part of the mechanism that performs that function.

Failure to feed could mean a failure of the shell carrier but, more likely, it's a dirty magazine tube. Who cleans inside the magazine? Hardly anyone. Vivenzio recommends using a ⅞ inch wooden dowel with a fine grit crocus cloth glued around one end to buff any rust or rough spots inside the magazine tube. A couple of times a year should be sufficient.

Failure to fire could mean a worn or broken firing pin but, more likely, grime and gritty oil has gummed up the works inside the bolt. You need to take the bolt down, clean and lightly oil it or, if the firing pin is short or broken, replace it.

Failure to extract could mean a broken extractor or extractor spring but, more likely, those gremlins of grime and grit are preventing the mechanical device from performing its function. A good cleaning is called for.

Failure to eject could mean a broken or bent ejector. In most guns this is a stationary structure, so grime and grit are usually not the problem.

These failures are rarely mechanical. If they are, they're problems to take to your armorer. Actually, they're more likely caused by a lack of tender loving care. If you depend on that shotgun to get you out of a tight situation, you want to be sure that the second shot will fire.

16.2 Disassembly and Cleaning

To get to the parts that need cleaning, you must know how to take the gun apart, but not so much that you get into trouble. I'm not going to bore you with instructions for each make and model shotgun; they're included in each package from the manufacturer. But the principles are basically the same.

Unscrew the magazine cap. Take off the barrel. Slide the fore-end forward gently, then depress the shell stop(s), so the action bars come out of the receiver. That exposes the bolt. Push out the one or two pins holding in the trigger group and it comes out as a unit. That's as far as you should go.

If your gun has a magazine extension, when you remove it the magazine spring and follower come out. If no extension, walk the pressure fit plug out of the end of the magazine tube with a screwdriver and remove the spring and

This disassembly procedure is typical. First, make sure the gun – in this case a Smith & Wesson Model 3000 – is unloaded; remove barrel. Then remove the pins holding the trigger group. *Bill Hill.*

The trigger assembly comes out as a unit. *Bill Hill.*

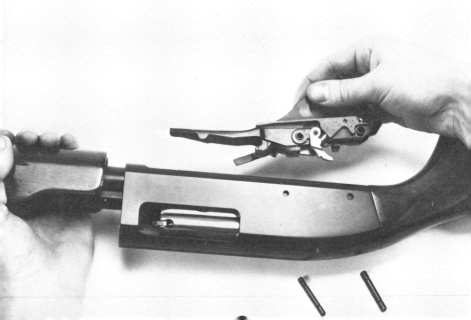

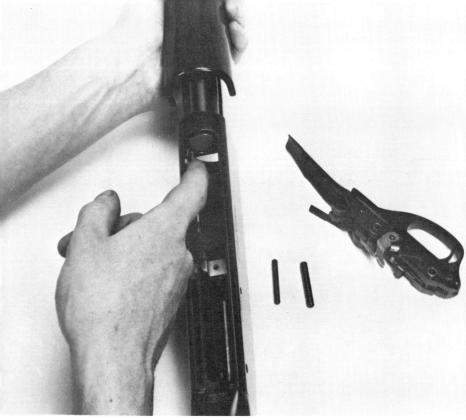

Depress shell stop so you can move slide forward . . . *Bill Hill*

and slide action bars and bolt out of the receiver. *Bill Hill*

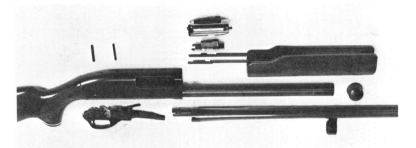

A Model 3000 pump gun field-stripped for cleaning. *Bill Hill*

follower. Cup your hand over the end to catch the spring when it's released. Now you can clean the inside of the magazine tube with that wooden dowel and crocus cloth. But don't oil it.

Clean the bolt, especially the face and around the extractor. Remember, one drop of oil is plenty. Clean the locking block and the locking notch in the barrel.

With the guts out of the shotgun, you can get inside the receiver to clean the shell stops, extractor, and rails that the action parts ride on. Again, one drop of oil.

The trigger assembly isn't as complicated as it looks, but mechanical problems are better left to your armorer. You can blow grit out of it with an air hose, or simply sweep it with a brush. If necessary, you can put a drop of oil around the hammer pivot and trigger pin. The oil will migrate around to where it's needed.

Then clean the bore of the barrel with a swab. If you use a cleaning solvent, swab the bore dry when you're finished. Okay, you can put in a *light* film of oil.

These are the points that should get attention when you do a thorough cleaning job on the gun. How often depends on the gun's environment. Humid climates demand more care against rust. If dust and dirt are in your air, you may need to clean out what has stuck to the oil inside. If you use too much oil, you'll need to clean it off.

16.3 Handy Tools

A simple tool kit can take care of any problem you might encounter with a shotgun. It should include:

- A ⅞ inch wooden dowel for cleaning the magazine tube.
- A 13mm socket on a long shaft for tightening the butt stock nut on the S&W, a long shaft screwdriver for a Remington.

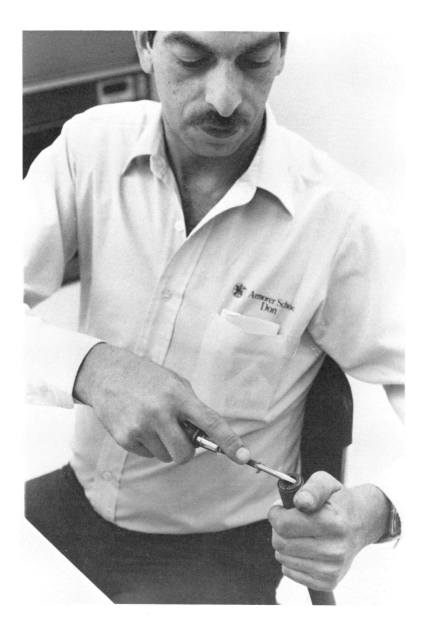

To clean the inside of the magazine tube, pry out the friction-fit plug at the end. The spring and plug will fly when they are free, so be careful.

S&W Armorer Don Vivenzio points out the extractor on the bolt. An old toothbrush helps here.

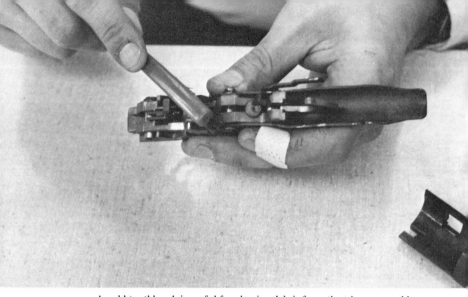

An old toothbrush is useful for clearing debris from the trigger assembly.

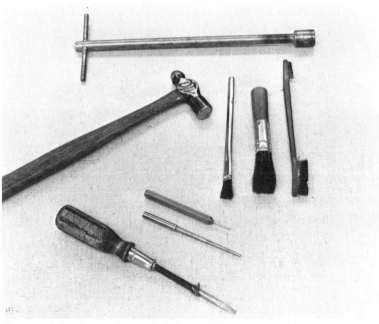

Handy tools for shotgun cleaning include a small hammer, screwdriver, a couple of drift pins, and a selection of brushes. That strange tool at top is simply a shaft welded onto a socket to tighten the butt stock nut on the Model 3000 shotgun.

- A nylon hammer eases removing some of the pins.
- A set of punches or drift pins.
- An India stone about 6 x ½ x ½ inches to smooth up rough surfaces. Never touch the sear or hammer notch unless you are an armorer.

16.4 Use Factory Service

It's usually easier to correct a problem by replacing an offending part. There's much your armorer can do to polish surfaces that ride against each other, straighten an action bar, and generally keep the gun in good working order.

There are certain things better left to the factory service station.

The ejector, in many guns, is staked into place. It isn't easily removed, nor does it often break.

Action bars are usually welded to a tube inside the fore-end (upper hand guard) so it's a "permanent" assembly. The factory can replace an action bar. But if it burns or cracks your fore-end, it must replace it — at no charge. If you ruin it, you'll have to buy a new assembly.

The magazine tube is a delicate part of the shotgun. If dented, it can hang up shells. It is probably threaded into the receiver, and is not easily removed. On some guns, it's virtually a permanent assembly. Repair or replacement of the magazine tube is also better left to factory service.

17

Concerns for Instructors

If a guy could load, unload, and spray a cardboard silhouette with buckshot, he was "qualified" with the shotgun. This history of inattention to the shotgun in police firearms training makes it difficult now to get the time it takes to instill good shotgun habits into someone who's likely fired one only at a cardboard silhouette. Yet this must be done, if we hope to prepare the officer for the day he searches the neighborhood for an armed felon.

17.1 Justifying a Shotgun Program

Too many municipalities believe the basic training every recruit receives at the state, regional, or big city training academy qualifies him forever. They don't realize that shooting methods and teaching techniques improve. Let's say your town just bought one brand and style of shotgun to replace the conglomerate congregation accumulated over the years. A couple of hours to familiarize the men with the new gun should be enough, shouldn't it?

No way.

Attorney Walter MacDonald, a firearms instructor with the Stoughton (Mass.) Police Department, tells me that two civil rights cases prove it isn't enough. You can use these citations to convince your town officials that a modest amount of money now is better than a judgment to the jugular later on.

Leite vs. City of Providence, 463 F. Supp. 585 (1978), held that the town, not just the officer, could be held liable for monetary damages if the plaintiff's injury resulted from non-existent or grossly inadequate training and supervision of a police department. This follows the "deep pockets" principle. The town has more money than an individual.

The bombshell dropped the following year with Popow vs. City of Margate, 476 F. Supp. 1237 (1979). This case involved the fatal shooting of an innocent bystander by a police officer. The decision applied the standards of the Leite case to the specific facts involved in the training of police officers by the city of Margate.

Officers customarily received recruit training at the State Police Academy. In-service training was conducted every six months at a local range.

However, there was no instruction on shooting at a moving target, night shooting, or shooting in residential areas. Margate is almost completely residential.

There was no training in the practical street applications of "shoot-don't shoot" law and policies. There was evidence that the police chief considered the rules of firing on residential streets to be a matter of "common sense," requiring no specific training.

The court held that such training could be held grossly inadequate and, therefore, the City of Margate would be liable.

"There were no exceptions for the 'we can't afford it' cities, nor for the 'it never happened before' towns," Walt MacDonald says. "Simply stated, municipalities were told they could spend now on training, or take a chance of spending a lot more later in damages."

17.2 A Positive Training Experience

Most of the students in your shotgun training class aren't there because they want to be. It's up to you to motivate them, to make it an enjoyable experience. You know how guys will compare scores on the handgun qualification course. Once you've done the indoctrination and familiarization, make a game of it. A little competition adds to the fun.

But be considerate of his shoulder. The number of rounds fired in training are probably the only shots your trainees will shoot with a shotgun. So why batter his brains out? You want him to *enjoy* this training experience. He'll become a better shotgun shooter sooner if he pays attention to the fundamentals, rather than concentrating on how hard that gun kicks him.

Use #9 target loads for training exercises. They're cheaper—and much easier on the shoulder.

You can introduce the heavier recoil of buck shot in an exercise that focuses attention on the target. Only when it's over, then point out to them that they were shooting a shell that supposedly kicks harder. Ask if they noticed. They'll probably say they didn't.

17.3 Looking Good

Muggers are the first to tell you they may pick their victims simply by the way they walk. If someone looks furtive, subjective or timid, they look like a victim. If you walk boldly and confidently, you look like someone *not* to be reckoned with.

Cops impart those same impressions. If they look unsure of themselves, or fumble with the shotgun, an aggressive subject may get the idea he could take that gun away. He probably could. But if they look proficient and confident, the perpetrator may think twice before he tries a gun grab.

So it's important that cops look good with their guns. That means getting enough range time for them to get really familiar with that shotgun.

17.4 Defending Your Training

Justify the content of your training program by designing it around the needs of your department. Study past shooting incidents; even incidents in which a shotgun could have been used, but wasn't. Define the challenge your men may face, then tailor your training to address those challenges. This makes your training program "relevant."

Keep copious records. Record every training session, complete with the lesson plan used. You may have to testify someday as to just what the officer was taught. Include not only his attendance record and qualification scores, but his proficiency in various exercises. In other words, record your impressions and evaluations of every student. Then you can testify from facts, rather than faulty memory.

18

References

18.1 Addresses of Companies Mentioned

AAI Corporation
P.O. Box 6767
Baltimore, MD 21204

Ballistic Research Industries
2825 Rodeo Gulch Road (#8)
Soquel, CA 95073

Browning
Route One
Morgan, UT 84050

Choate Machine & Tool Co.
P.O. Box 218
Bald Knob, AR 72010

Federal Cartridge Corp.
2700 Foshay Tower
Minneapolis, MN 55402

F.I.E.
4530 N.W. 135th Street
Opa-Lacka, FL 33054

Heckler & Koch
14601 Lee Road
Chantilly, VA 22021

Hi-Caliber Products
666 Dundee Road (#1607)
Northbrook, IL 60062

Ithaca Gun Company
123 Lake Street
Ithaca, NY 14850

Michaels of Oregon Co.
P.O. Box 13010
Portland, OR 97213

O. F. Mossberg & Sons
7 Grasso Street
North Haven, CT 06473

Sound-Off Safety, Inc.
5300 Madison Ave.
Hudsonville, MI 49426

North American Ordnance Corp.
1856 Star-Batt Drive
Rochester, MI 48063

Special Weapons Products
Space Center (Bldg. 601)
Mira Loma, CA 91752

Remington Arms Co.–Du Pont
Wilmington, DE 19898

Trius Products
P.O. Box 25
Cleveland, OH 45002

Sage International
1856 Star-Batt Drive
Rochester, MI 48063

U.S. Repeating Arms Co.
P.O. Box 30-300
New Haven, CT 06511

Savage Industries
Springdale Road
Westfield, MA 01085

Winchester Group-Olin
120 Long Ridge Road
Stamford, CT 06904

18.2 Addresses and Telephone Numbers of Training Specialists

Massad Ayoob
Lethal Force Institute
P.O. Box 122
Concord, NH 03301
603-224-6814

Libby Callahan, Executive Director
International Association of Law
    Enforcement Firearms Instructors
P.O. Box 47015
Forestville, MD 20747-7015
301-735-1974

John S. Farnum
Defense Training, Inc.
P.O. Box 665
Niwot, CO 80544-0665
303-530-7106

Robert K. Lindsey, Director
Organizational and Individual
    Development
Wells Fargo Guard Services
800 Commerce Road West
Harahan, LA 70123
504-734-4308

Robert E. Hunt, Director
Smith & Wesson Academy
P.O. Box 2208
Springfield, MA 01102-2208
413-781-8300 (Ext. 255)